MW01099094

RUDOLPH VALENTINO
THE UNTOLD STORY

WAYNE VINCENT HATFORD

Whitley Heights Publishing
San Francisco, CA
www.valentinospeaks.com

TABLE OF CONTENTS

Not every person or event in Rudy's life is going to be addressed in these pages. The contents reflect what he considers to have the most potential to enlighten the reader.

INTRODUCTION

R udolph Valentino wants to get personal here, give us his take on some of the people and events that colored his life, especially during his heyday in Hollywood. As with our previous collaborations, I am honored to have acted as scribe and present this material, unexpurgated. What you will read is exactly what Rudy wants to convey, how he sees things now, from the Other Side!

Over the years much has been written about Valentino's life, both fact and fiction. The contents of this book, 'write' from the horse's mouth, aim to correct the record as well as reveal that which has never been revealed before. This is the real Rudy, reflections on an era as seen through his own lens.

Everything in quotes has been channeled, sourced from the spirit essence of Rudolph Valentino. All other remarks, as indicated by the use of italics, are mine.

~ Wayne Vincent Hatford

"The ultimate value of this work is belief and the soul's progress to serve its purpose."

~ RVG

FOREWORD

"I was never much for gossip, in any arena, and especially not where my own wings were being singed as they have been on numerous occasions. Even so, there are some stories that need to be told. My goal in doing so is to be instructive, to share my recollections in order to help illumine your own pathways. That this may be accomplished is my greatest legacy, the culmination of my trajectory as a star."

~ *Rudolph Valentino*

ACKNOWLEDGMENTS

"Dedicato alla mia famiglia, agli amici, amanti, estimatori, appassionati ~ a quelli che hanno seguito, da sempre, il percorso della mia anima. Vi ringrazio, tutti quanti, e sopratutto Wayne, per la sua dedizione ed il suo sforzo in questo lavoro: mettere per iscritto con la sua penna le mie parole. Beati voi!"

~ *Rodolfo Valentino*

(Dedicated to my family, friends, lovers, fans ~ to those who, from the beginning of time, have followed my soul's journey. I thank all of you, and especially Wayne, for his dedication and effort in this work: putting my words to paper with his pen. Light and Love!)

THEOREM

"Every life-time is a mosaic. While in it, we meet a plethora of people, each one an energy field which, in combination with our own, continually create cause and effect, or as some might say, drama. In sharing about people I knew and some of my experiences with them, I hope to provide you with a better understanding of catalysts and how they contribute to our growth. Sure, we learn from our environments and the social mores that surround us, but we learn the most from the people we interact with, for good or ill!"

~ RVG

There were a number of players in Rudy's life who impacted his evolution, both as a movie-star and man. Here are some of the more notable ones, aggregated by category.

FAMILY & EARLY YEARS

GABRIELLE BARBIN GUGLIELMI (*mother*)

"No one could have ever been sweeter, more caring, more astute, where I was concerned! My mother, an angel in the flesh, knew who I was down to the smallest detail. She knew my moods, foibles, what made me tick. Of course, because of the familial nature of our relationship, we had limits on how close we could be. But we melded on the energetic level, in the mind. Karmically we were here to spark each other. It was because of Gabrielle that I dreamed what I dreamt, becoming known, although for what was a mystery when I was young. And my task with her was to keep her engaged. She never found me boring although she could predict some of my choices.

A symbiosis like no other, ever more. Yes, we are still in vibration on the Other Side, and we continue our work together, which I would describe as a certain mutuality involving mentoring. Yes, my mother was a mentor in life as I was for her, what most people did not realize about our dynamic as it was cloaked in the mother/son construct. Gabrielle was an exemplary mother, to me, also to my siblings. We were all very fond of her and what she had to offer/proffer. Everyone loved her. She exuded joy in even the smallest of activities."

ALBERTO GUGLIELMI VALENTINO (*brother*)

"**Mon frère aîné**. (*My older brother.*) He always thought himself wiser, the sage, as this was a stance promulgated by our father. So he maintained a distance but not a separation. He was eternally available to dispense counsel when we needed or wanted it, Maria and I. Actually, he had a bit more interaction with and influence on Maria and her life decisions than mine. I loved my brother and he me but we were not openly affectionate. Slightly stiff yet warm and cordial are the adjectives I would apply to our meetings of the mind and body. I was appreciative of who he was and secretly he was proud of me, of my renown, and by extension the **gloire** (*glory*) he felt our family deserved. He carried the hint of nobility that distinguished all the Guglielmis, di Valentina.

How he cried, Alberto, when I passed! He was briefly inconsolable and bereft. For the sake of his son and wife, however, he quickly recovered and played his role as **paterfamilias**. (*Head of the family.*) I do wish he had had a penchant for the silver screen but alas he did not and was not really welcomed in that sphere where he was viewed not as his own man but in my shadow."

MARIA GUGLIELMI STRADA (*sister*)

"**La mia sorella!** (*My sister!*) What a dear, sweet soul who reflected so many of our mother's traits, her clear-eyed, steely appraisals, industriousness, and penchant for providing me with an audience. Yes, Maria was my first **claque**, (*group of devoted fans*) of one! It was she I often wanted to astonish as a child, with my feats and flights of fancy. I would recite to her as though I was on stage, and she observed my frequent lapses of good judgment, also, upon occasion, a tinge of foolhardiness. Maria was a kind sort, wanting the best for both of her brothers, as we did for her. We, she and I, however, had a special bond, apart from our familial connections with Alberto. She was not as enamored as he with my later success, never saw me in the spotlight really, though I had already claimed it as a youth. How we entertained each other as children, she being the proxy for our mother, the loving and careful eye!

Oh Maria, I hoped you would have had more opportunity to shine. Not that you didn't, but a woman of your time in Italy was subject to certain constraints. In summation, I love you, always have, always will, and our connection remains a viable one. Yes, that means we continue to have truck, a state of being that is likely to continue indefinitely. A life well-lived! **Bravo, dico!**" (*I salute you!*)

JEAN VALENTINO (*nephew*)

"He embodied certain aspects of his grandfather and father, not so much Gabrielle or his mother. The supposition he was mine, my son and not my nephew, is false. He was the issue of my brother, pure and simple. I wanted to lighten him up a little as he was a serious child who needed to have his creativity engaged. But, he became, as you know, an excellent sound engineer, editor, his ear (and eye) keen on what was needed or wanted in each production. I wish we could have interacted a bit more but distance and time intervened and Jean needed to be in Europe when young to learn what later provided him with impetus, namely his attention to detail. Love to him. We do communicate in spirit, and to all who descend from him, who honor our name and blood line in a variety of ways, **je suis fier de vous, Gabrielle est fière de vous!** (*I am proud of you; Gabrielle is proud of you!*) We wish you Light, Love, and great understanding!

Rodolfo Valentino, **celui qui vous aime!**" (*He who loves you!*)

GIOVANNI GUGLIELMI (*father*)

"About my father I can shed no new light and our interactions were not, in retrospect, exemplary though at least cogent and perfunctory."

RUDY ON HIS FRENCH ROOTS

"Let's stipulate that I am/was half French to begin with and my mother had strongly embraced that language and culture, brought them to Italy with her, saw them as a trophy throughout her life. She delighted in speaking French to us as children. It was our own flavor, our refuge, something she thought would make us more able in the world. This is not to say that she did not love Italy, Puglia in particular. Anyway, French, in all its ramifications, seeped into our lives and we thought it grand, saw our capability with it as an **entrée**. (*Door-opener.*) So when I went to Paris during my teen-age years to, in fact, sow wild oats, try out the **boulevardier** (*man about town*) premise, I summoned my French parts, made them shine, and gathered my forces which later translated to the continental flair I was known to display as aspects of screen characters I embodied.

That we read in French, novels and history in particular, was a really nurturing part of my upbringing. Did I like the precision of French in composition? Not so much as a boy yet I was a sponge. I knew that language inside out, and admired the elegance inherent in the culture. **Le Comte** (*Count*) Valentino, perhaps an alter ego? Oh the excesses I knew while in the thrall of my first visit to Paris! How dandy it all was!"

CASTELLANETA AND TARANTO

"These two cities were the bookends of my youth, the proscenium arches where my plays were started, also where I became a man. The ravine versus the seaside, two very different environments in close proximity and both impacted who I became. One not better than the other; rather, both were and continue to be memorable, crammed with sights, sounds, experiences, adventures, fantasies, and the people who made them tick, grease for the goose, and gander."

(*Rudy's birthplace, Via Roma, 116, Castellaneta, Italy.*)

IN-LAWS

'MUZZIE' AND RICHARD HUDNUT
(Natacha's mother and step-father)

"Was I ever dazzled by their wealth, **ébloui** as the French might say? Of course, but not in any duplicitous way and never with any particular goal in mind. I enjoyed watching them revel in their riches, that's all, just as I did in my own ~ whenever I could! I never sought their largesse and neither was it offered, except in small doses such as tokens of appreciation and hospitality. Our relations had a **gemütlich** (*comfortable*) quality to them, a generosity of spirit, which is what I really valued."

TERESA WERNER *(Natacha's aunt, friend)*

"This lady was my surrogate mother, also an advisor, a kind soul who wanted the best for her niece, and me. She saw us in our glory as a couple and did her utmost to perpetuate that glow, which I have made reference to before. Teresa had an inherent wisdom that allowed her to befriend only those who were truly worthy of her company. And she was adventuresome, while doing it in a matronly way. So cute, so loved her dearly, and we conspired, huddled, ̲rred, often.

Natacha sometimes thought why not Rudy and my Aunt? They are the perfect couple! Indeed, we were quite compatible but, of course, the physical was not there, not dreamed of either. The meeting of the minds, however, what a delight, what bravura! Steely good sense too. **Ti amo** (*I love you*) Teresa! She remains in spirit and is one of my dearest confidants, even to this present time."

FRIENDS & ACQUAINTANCES

R*udy was known for his free and easy manner. Indeed, he was always approachable, even in his loftiest days as a star. As for friendships, he preferred them to be a fair exchange, to give as much as he got, receive as much as he offered.*

JUNE MATHIS (*screenwriter, friend*)

"June, when it really counted, had my back and she, perhaps to a greater extent than anyone else, Natacha included, was able to perceive my spark, my soul ⁓ if you will, the core being. So she knew I could handle whatever a script might suggest, overtly, and inwardly. A lover of the golden mean, it was as though June filled a syringe and injected truth into her body of work. What it contained was pure Light!

I was one of the people who inspired her, encouraged her to go farther, to stretch what people held as their own truths. June had a tremendous drive, which seemed rather low-key when you interacted with her, yet upon reading her treatments people were amazed at her precision, facility with a plot.

She did have a soft spot in her heart for me, also for my home country, which impinged upon her personal choices such as the man she married. June and I had a shorter arc of time to work with than most people and she fulfilled a pact she made with herself: to spread consciousness, play with that elasticity. I do regret that late in our life-times there was static, a misunderstanding about the script for "*The Hooded Falcon.*" Some of that was based on a power struggle between two creative women, both of whom had great contributions to make. I loved June's adventuresome spirit, her willingness to explore the Great Beyond, her support on so many levels. A sterling soul, Ms. Mathis, who in the 1920's film industry had wind in her sails, blazed many trails!"

Rudy, did you attend séances with June Mathis?

"Yes, I did indeed attend a few with her, voice mediums and more informal gatherings where we called out to those on the Other Side, imploring them to respond. And talk they did, though not always in complete sentences. June was quite a fan of automatic writing, a 'seraphine' of sorts. Had an angelic voice too, her inner self I mean, in tune with the Ages. It was old hat for her, that sort of work."

ANABEL HENDERSON (*acquaintance*)

"She and I were friends, first and foremost, though more in passing. She definitely was not one of my more significant encounters but she was tactful, something I appreciated about her, and without guile. She wanted nothing from me but to make my acquaintance and then explore it. So explorations there were but none registered that strongly on either of our psyches. Those articles, the ones she wrote many years after the fact: someone encouraged her to make a little money ~ a certain degree of embellishment, therefore, in the content. A lovely woman, sweet disposition, fashionable."

NORMAN KERRY (*film actor, friend*)

"Of my male friends less is known as I did not elaborate, expound on their characters or the quality of our interactions much when last I walked the Earth. Norman was a special case as there was a sense that all was possible when he and I were in proximity. We inspired and encouraged each other in the career arena, and Norman had a quiet drive, no tilt-a-whirl was he ~ very focused and salt of the earth.

What I liked most about him is that I could trust him as a friend. Swell that we conspired to be successful together, egged each other on and I will avow there was, and continues to be, to this day, a brotherly flavor in all our communications. We were also quite practical in our flights of fancy, and the 'potential' building blocks we bandied about were grounded in the true veracity of their origins. We drifted in and out of each other's lives and though intimate in a platonic sense we could also be happy for each other by being apart. Nothing out of whack here, no excessive gravitas, just sincere!"

PAUL IVANO (*cameraman, friend*)

"One of my most trusted confidants, he was eyes and ears for so many of the happenings in my life, what you would call in today's jargon a 'fair witness,' except that he primarily looked through the lens of a camera rather than with the naked eye. So interesting that Natacha was almost as comfortable with his presence as I. The three of us shared a living space for a time and that was never a problem. Indeed, we were respectively quite respectful of who and what we were, individually and in coordination with each other.

Paul became far less prominent in my life as my star continued to rise but we were never completely out of touch. There were hiatuses, however, and that was fine with both of us.

I liked his style, adjunct, yes, but also commanding when the situation called for it. A true friend, he remained faithful to our friendship for the balance of his life-time. Mundanely, he got me excited about all things visual and, unbeknownst to him, he also helped me hone my craft, him on one side of the camera and me on the other. Dear Paul, **grazie mille**! (*Many thanks!*) He has returned to the flesh but we continue our rapport, me functioning as one of his guides, a thank you for his rock-steady support.

Keen on everything was Paul, one of the most agreeable people I ever encountered. Lights, camera, action, those were his three favorite words!"

DOUGLAS GERRARD (*actor, director, friend*)

"I suppose you could describe him as a wing man. He was a bystander, yes, sometimes, but also someone who participated, showing up at several important junctures in my life. Palm Springs figured in the equation as well as my ill-fated marriage, the second, which was the first to Natacha, our union in Mexico. Douglas often ran interference, meaning he had my back or was a willing initiator on my behalf. We shared a love of creativity and spent many an hour weighing options, day-dreaming. He rode horses too, which is something we did together in the desert.

Not as deep of a connection as I had with some others but I valued his perceptions and his ability to be a practical ally, someone who always knew what to do. 'Wise counselor' would sum up the role he played and that is how I saw him. He had more career notoriety later, just dandy with me. I urged him to invest in himself, to recognize his strengths. Again, a peer kind of friendship where we ran scenarios, courses of action. He also introduced me to a number of playful, inventive people. A **macher** (*doer*) he was, go-to kind of guy. Full of the Irish also, which implies a certain amount of agility, the art of being supple, quicksilver."

ANDRE DAVEN (*aspiring actor, friend*)

"That so much time is still being taken up by people speculating about my personal life is amazing! No one could know, ever, when and to what extent I was motivated by my rapport with any particular individual, unless you were able to walk in my shoes!

I experienced closeness with some of the male persuasion, par for the course for just about every man ~ that is clear. Now, what people want to make of it is not. Natacha and I had our own ways of being. André was an acolyte, someone with whom I developed a liking but it was not destined for import or even to be that remarkable. I could describe him as a good-time Charlie, very agreeable and eager to learn about the film industry. Yes, I did get him a little screen time in "*Monsieur Beaucaire*," to give him a taste of the ecstasy involved with being in front of a camera and for this he was eternally grateful. Earnest yet apprehensive, he

19

needed reassurance and it was the earnest part I found rewarding, what inspired me to take him under my wing, act as mentor. We also shared a lot, sometimes talked for hours about our impressions of the world, within and without. He was a good listener and in return he got a few tips from me.

Again, much has been made of our friendship yet it was not all that significant, and certainly not what it has been purported to be. We were fellow thespians acting out roles. That is the essence, how best to describe this interaction. Then, like moth to a flame, André went up in smoke, literally taking a powder."

FRANK MENNILLO (*family friend, mentor*)

"I will address him but primarily not to muse or recollect but simply to clarify our relationship which was perfunctory. Pleasant yes, but duty-tinged. As you may well know, his role was one of theoretical godfather, the person who was supposed to show me the ropes in the new world. Well, what he revealed was not exactly to my liking as I did not feel I needed to be rich for that sake alone, as did he. When I had made a name for myself, Frank wanted to hitch a ride on the glamour train, again, duty-bound, always wanting to set me straight, according to his standards which I found mired in the myopic mysteries of mendacity. He was a 'means to an end' kind of guy and his tutelage added a note of caution. He provided me with contrast, made me more aware of elements in my own make-up that I neither wanted to pursue or emphasize.

Did Frank teach me the ways of the world, how to dress, interact with polite society? No, friends, these I learned through connections, friendships, opportunities that I was able to manifest of my own accord. Did he attempt to influence me, paint me with his own varnish? Yes, indeed, but it did not stick! These, essentially, are the key elements of my interactions with Frank. By the way, he was not one of Natacha's favorites!"

MANUEL REACHI (*diplomat, writer, producer, bon vivant, friend*)

"Someone with whom I had a lot of contact, but not always the most beneficial kind. In today's parlance Manuel was an enabler and he often colluded with my baser instincts, especially my adventures with women where there was no chance of the interaction being anything but sexual. Agnes Ayres married him, you know, and the fact that we were friends, he and I, encouraged her to drop her guard.

Manuel and I often spoke Spanish and that was how I gradually improved my capabilities with that language. We met before my star began to soar and then, when it did, Manuel became somewhat of a hanger-on. Of course, he had his own connections but I would have to describe him as a bit of a gadfly. Never a cross word between us as he always encouraged me to indulge/overindulge. I did very much appreciate his savoir-faire and ability to work a room."

ROBERT FLOREY (*writer, publicist, actor, director, friend*)

"Another buddy, Monsieur Robert, **molto fine come persona**. (*A very refined person.*) He riled my French parts meaning there was a slightly confrontational or combative nature to our interactions - all in good fun, however, and in pursuit of intellectual stimulation. We, of course, would

French-ify some of our discussions, throw a Gallic wrench into the mix now and again. He sometimes fronted for me, was what you now call a point man, plying publicity that touted me, or highlighted my roles in films, and had a long and varied career himself.

Robert admired my prowess and was often present when I was involved in some kind of sport. He was a bit covetous in that he wished he could package some musculature for himself. But this was innocent, part of his boyish charm. He looked up to me yet he did not brook, stood his ground intellectually, always. Robert, **je te souviens fort bien**! (*I remember you well!*) In summation, he was a confidant and true friend. I count myself lucky to have had a few, which is more than most men!"

FEDERICO BELTRAN-MASSES (*artist, friend*)

"We met in my latter days without, naturally, my being aware that this was so. This was a romance, not physically, but in the sense that I fell in love with his work, the art that issued forth from his hands by way of his eyes, for they were keen observers. Federico was a worldly man, unattractive in the traditional manner, yet his vibrancy called out, to patrons and public alike. His style caught the mood of the 1920's, expressed it perfectly. I was honored he wanted to paint me and sought out my company.

There is a story he found me with a gun, wanting to kill myself. I certainly did own a gun, more than one, but I did not contemplate doing myself in so I refute that notion. I do avow, however, that Federico may have had a perception of such but that was literally fanciful on his part. We were lovers of 'luxe' (*luxury*) ~ anything of refined or rarified taste, from cigars to cars, and his flavor, that of Europe, I found to be an elixir, something I sought to drink of, and often. The combination, he and I, equaled great collaboration. This was a fated exchange and we are at peace with it; nothing further needs to occur."

GEORGE ULLMAN (*business manager, friend*)

"A fine fellow he seemed and he did have a lot of expertise in paying attention to transactions, meaning he saw beyond the obvious and had a good nose for a buck, the latter, especially, a rather important quality for anyone who would aspire to do well in such a position. Now his judgment, sometimes, got clouded with his own ambition. And he over-identified with my career, how he thought it should unfold. Bottom line, he meddled a bit, with good intentions mostly, but they did sometimes lean towards the evidence of ego. Mr. Ullman was not bereft of ego though he would say he did it all for me, to promulgate and perpetuate my myth, the one that he and Hollywood had jointly conspired to create. We had a karmic tie and I surrendered to what I perceived his wisdom to be, not always, but upon occasion.

George became a Valentino in his own mind. He lived and breathed my memory post departure. Indeed, my death may have affected him even more than my family, Natacha, or any number of friends. Do not get me wrong, George was a savior but he was also somewhat of a manipulator. Love to him and we still have things to sort out. In spirit we have been able to interact and review our time together. Much of what George wrote about later was embellished, which he did for me, for my image, to burnish what was already polished. No need, but he felt there was. Though my life-time spoke for itself, he thought he should add a few flourishes.

Steady as she goes ~ as a manager, he was an expert at sailing my ship."

LUTHER MAHONEY (*employee, friend*)

"Mr. Fix-it, that man had an uncanny understanding of the mechanical, a quality I found particularly endearing. That is why we hired him, engaged him in our employ. And, he was rather discrete. No running to newspapers to talk about what Natacha, or I, ate for breakfast. He was a focused person, jack of all trades. He could wear lots of hats, all very well. Oddly, I sometimes sought his advice, and even where his frames of reference did not allow him to offer any, his presence, steadfastness, led me to formulate my own conclusions. Luther: a really good-hearted soul, always with a smile and kind demeanor."

JACQUES HEBERTOT (*Paris theater director, acquaintance*)

"**Artiste chez les artistes, très accueillant ce monsieur!** (*An artist among artists, he was very welcoming!*) We, Natacha and I, sought out those who contributed to the glory of art, whether in theater, as was the case with Jacques, or cinema, or any other arena. Monsieur also wanted to rub elbows with the Valentinos so there was mutuality in our interactions and we enjoyed them immensely. We were treated like royalty and very properly, I might add. No one took any liberties they ought not to have, on any level. Jacques is not someone I knew well yet there was natural camaraderie afoot, as was the case with Mrs. Valentino. She found him quite amusing, our **entrée** (*ticket*) into the world of French theater. A feather in our respective caps, and he took such delight in our presence!"

ROLF DE MARE (*director of the Swedish ballet in Paris, acquaintance*)

"A minor player although intriguing in his own right. **Maître de danse**, very talented impresario; I did not know him well, however. A few evenings in his company which were grand, glorious champagne-sotted affairs, revels in the City of Light."

SERGE DIAGHILEV (*director of the Ballets Russes in Paris, acquaintance*)

"I had the good fortune to attend the Ballets Russes on two occasions, during my first visit to Paris when Nijinsky graced the stage, and again, years later. That is why I had no hesitation in acceding to Natacha's wishes when she expressed an interest in seeing me photographically arrayed in said dancer's full regalia, though lots of it was paint! The night we met, Monsieur Diaghilev held forth with great charm and wit, filling the room with his effusive charisma. **Dans les prunelles de ses yeux, on voyait danser ses lubies qui oscillaient comme le mercure.** (*His eyes truly reflected his mercurial nature.*) Quite the visionary and arbiter of taste, his world was steeped in culture."

(*Serge's niece, Tamara Diaghilev, is a friend, teacher, and mentor to me. I am extremely grateful for her presence in my life.*)

ENRICO CARUSO (*opera singer, acquaintance*)

"**Ci siamo conosciuti, lui ed io, a New York.** (*We met in New York.*) His fame was legendary long before then so imagine my thrill to be able to shake hands and talk with such a marvelous entertainer, he who sang from his soul, to touch those of other people. We conversed in Italian of course, chatted about life, its twists and turns, and the business of opera and other stage craft. He was resolute in his commitment to art, a quality I sought to emulate.

So amusing that certain newspapers, and others, wanted to see us together in the Great Beyond fraternizing in our Italian-ness, soon after my passing. Indeed, photos were contrived that purported to show just that. **Che buffo!**" (*How funny!*)

GEORGE WEHNER (*medium, post-death acquaintance*)

"This gentleman was unknown to me during my life-time as Rudy yet he was instrumental in my growth, gave me voice almost immediately after my passing, solidifying my efforts to assuage and reassure Natacha and to support agreements we had made, unspoken, that because we both believed in the Hereafter and communicated with those in the Great Beyond ourselves that so should it be possible for me to do the same thing, which it was, and is.

Natacha was comforted by Wehner's work, his messages from me and, as you know, she incorporated some of them into the book she published following my death. Wehner was an empath very well suited to his profession, able to sensitize himself to any entity in question. He showed me I could speak ~ the silent star that had, and still has, a lot to say! In those first transmissions I was very much in shock so they were not as clear as I am now or have been via other mediums in the intervening years. Suffice to say Wehner was a good choice and he and Natacha had strong rapport. She felt confident about his abilities, and was not disappointed.

Now, or rather more recently, George and I have conversed about the nature of trans-dimensional communication, especially writing, as we are doing tonight. Alignments have occurred, in general and in particular, that make it even easier now for me to accomplish. (*Speaking to the author*) This is true for you also!"

MAE WEST (*stage and film actress, post-death acquaintance*)

"She wanted to meet me in the worst way, smitten with my image, and of course I was aware of hers, being what it was during her time on stage. We almost accomplished that goal at a promotional party given to honor the release of "*Son of the Sheik*" ~ almost, because we missed each other by minutes. And then she heard of my hasty departure from this world and wept. Yes, she of the constructed quips voicing what others would like to say, given half a chance. But Mae's take was unique and often very funny! So she attempted to establish a friendship with me and did, post-death, calling upon several mediums over the years to reach out, say my name. Therefore, I confirm we did interact though not when both in the flesh.

We have looked each other up since, however, in the NOW, and she is the pip she always was. Her sparkle has not waned. So there you have it, Miss West and I, two unlikely souls, played a role in each other's lives. To be frank, she would have wanted some Rudy and I might well have acquiesced, glitter and diamonds notwithstanding."

HARRY HOUDINI (*magician, post-death acquaintance*)

"My compatriot, in that we both generated notoriety though obviously for vastly different reasons. Harry manipulated reality and so did I, through picture plays presented on the screen. His work was live, so to speak, and in that sense particularly enthralled his fans. He had a love/hate for the Great Beyond, entering it at times to perform tricks and cast illusions yet fearing his own passing, the latter not really a problem for me. (Some trepidation there was, I will say in parenthesis, but not fears.)

Anyway, Mr. Houdini was a special type and that he continues to be. We have had confabs in our present experiences with life, reviewed together, which some of you call peer counseling. He and I have rapport though we personally did not meet up in that life-time, as Harry and Rudy. He honored my essence, however, with his presence at my funeral only months before his own scheduled departure.

How he tweaked the proscenium arch, tantalized audiences, made them gasp, with his feats! Harry, you were the man, the magic purveyor par excellence!"

LESLIE FLINT (*medium, post-death acquaintance*)

"Mr. Flint had quite a strong personality of his own which never completely abated when he was in trance so my observation and experience is that he did not fully step aside, at least not when he channeled me. This is not to say I was a false Rudy in those circumstances, just not a completely unfettered one. Now he did give me voice and much practice over the ether. I grew more and more comfortable communicating with those in the flesh during his sojourn on the Earth Plane. And, I was able to be helpful, through him, to large numbers of people. So thank you, Leslie! We have spoken in spirit by the way. Our connection is deep, founded upon the interactions we had in several incarnations.

Leslie popularized mediumistic communication, normalized it as well, and for this he deserves kudos."

(Nita Naldi, the quintessential vamp, with Rudy in "Cobra"
~ Ritz-Carlton/Paramount, 1925)

CO·STARS

O ne of the great intangibles in the movie business, but oh
so important, is who will be cast with whom. Rudy was
fortunate to work with a number of capable leading ladies,
including Gloria Swanson.

NITA NALDI (film actress, friend, intimate)

"This woman was one of the best foils any actor could ever
have! We were opposites but that allowed us to compliment
each other. Attractive but not pretty in a conventional way,
she could convey the most nefarious mannerisms, vamp-like
behavior that was thoroughly, and morally, bankrupt. Nita
and I were great buddies and the rumors are true. We did
once explore when everything seemed new. Then we had a
laugh about it later, curiosity having paid its due. Without
Nita to support me, I could not have mastered those roles as
effectively as I did. She was an icon and, of course, the
women in the audience were not threatened by our kisses,
knowing that we would not truly succumb.

Nita was the archetype of temptation every time we
appeared together on the screen. In real life, however, she

was blasé, never took Hollywood too seriously, yet grateful that her look, and demeanor, were so perfect for the moment. I remember her fondly. Love, Rodolfo."

MAE MURRAY (*film actress, friend, lover*)

"Vivacious, sumptuous, this is what she exuded on a personal level. It was like she wanted to take care of you which, in my case, she most certainly did. We fell into an easy rapport that lasted for a number of years. Conferring confabs, and the occasional tryst for yes, we were intimate from time to time, depending on what was extant in our other personal and public endeavors. Lots of champagne flowed, lots of flowers in the room! Accoutrements, you could say, were important elements to both Mae and I. Her beauty was undeniable, and I partook, **comme je vous ai dit**, (*as I have told you*) in a similar way, as a honey bee deposits in the hive. Mae, the Queen Bee, for that is the analogy that speaks to the heart of her personhood. Were we close companions? Not as much as cohorts who occasionally cavorted."

DOROTHY GISH (*film actress, friend*)

"We worked together on a picture (*"Nobody Home/Out of Luck"*) that unfortunately is lost. I did cherish that experience for I found her character and, indeed, her physical presence, so uplifting. She was clarity incarnated, a mirror, who reflected in her role, whatever it was, with perfect pitch and acuity. Dorothy was blessed with a talented sister, as you know, whose name was greater than hers in terms of fame but of this she thought not, did not even consider it in her calculations. She was Miss Gish to me on set but Doro in person. We had a familial relationship, warm, friendly, engaging. What a lovely individual! Nothing to disassemble or figure out ~ pure bliss! Am so happy we met, also that we had an opportunity to silver screen it, shoot a film together. And, she was partial to hats in the sense that she got me to pay attention to them long before I met Natacha who was so smitten with chapeaux. Funny how these little echoes tend to repeat themselves in every life!"

GLORIA SWANSON (*film actress, friend*)

"My darling co-star! How we pranked each other, almost every day, and in every way! What creativity our endeavors did require! She was so much fun to work with and she did not consider me an inferior, not Miss Swanson, she of the 'glorified' heights! Her career was at a summit, somewhat akin to the one portrayed in our film (*"Beyond the Rocks."*) Her eyes sparkled, winked a lot, as we took the scenario, tongue in cheek. This saved the production actually as the audience reacted to our levity in a positive way. Had we been too serious, we could have easily gotten the hook.

Gloria and I did not broach intimacy, knowing, as we did, that that move would have been disastrous. Instead, we rode, in motorcars, and on horses, were friends who understood the most intricate aspects of each other's psyches without having to have direct experiences with them. Bravo, Gloria! You were always a **tour de force!**"

VILMA BANKY (*film actress, friend*)

"A treasure trove, Miss Banky, and I did not immediately realize how many facets she actually had, far more even than were displayed in the two films we shared on the screen. The definition of a model leading lady who contributed greatly to the all-around success of both those efforts! I soothed her slightly jangled sensibilities, those that were exacerbated by being in a land where her communication skills were limited. I brought out her glow, the ease upon which she hung her characterizations. We were not physical or lusty with each other, yet we were able to portray those possibilities on film. Vilma reflected goodness to audiences and they thought 'what a perfect match' for my characters, my roles in those scripts. Compassion was the main ingredient; we had a rapport based on this most sacred of human behaviors: to be able to empathize with one another.

On a practical level, Vilma and I mostly communicated in French, a language she was fairly proficient in. And given that Hungarian was Greek to me that was our only option. Studio brass thought Miss Banky ideal in our pairing and indeed they were correct, she was. Two of my best celluloid efforts or should I say nitrate! Easy shoots, synchronicity spiced with **élan** (*impetus*) ~ **je t'aime** (*I love you*) Vilma!

We are not in contact now but we shall have another life in close proximity, and so it is written!"

AGNES AYRES (*film actress, friend*)

"My co-conspirator, for that is how we felt and even remarked upon while constructing the 'Sheik' films. We exchanged pregnant glances off set and sometimes on, when demanded by the director. Some would say my performance as the Sheik was eye-popping and it was that at times, again as the director so required. But, all in good fun!

34

Agnes was both very down to earth and quite a proper lady, though she also did not blush when there was a slightly risqué joke being shared. She and I discussed our roles a fair amount, especially during the second outing. I lament the chagrins she faced with her husband and personal life. Post-Sheiks, she apparently was high strung and had some difficulties reconciling her reality. This was not foreshadowed in our interactions; I was unaware of it at the time.

Agnes so graciously returned, as you know, for a small role in "*Son of the Sheik*." I think our work together was solid and I shall forever be indebted to her for a great deal of my success or rather how I most impressed the public, which was in this vehicle, not my preferred means of conveyance but ultimately rather effective. There was never any romance between us yet we were able to play at that, hint of its existence in how we comported with each other. She remains in spirit but we are not in touch at the moment. Dear Agnes, such a formal name! She found herself in a position of great envy, breathing life into Mrs. Hull's confection."

ALICE TERRY (*film actress*)

"Though she was reluctant as an actress, this trait is what made her shine, helped her stand out from the crowd, casting or cattle call. That she had a husband (*Rex Ingram*) who wielded a certain amount of power at Metro, later MGM, was also very helpful for her career. But to return to Alice's attributes, this reticence imbued her with a touch of innocence and wide-eyed devotion. Alice and I worked together twice, very smoothly I might add. Whatever her husband thought of it was purely a figment of his imagination.

I owe Alice a lot; she provided me with a perfect counterpart/counterweight for my role as Julio, she of the angelic countenance. Our looks, though opposite, were also complimentary, as were the feelings emanating from and evoked by our roles. Alice, you were not particularly generous with your words later in life, found fault, yet we shown, sparkled, in "*The Four Horsemen*," exhibiting acumen beyond our respective years. We have had truck, she and I, in the spirit world, and we are fine, no extraneous variables to repair. Mirrors, we were, in both of the films we did together. Love, Rodolfo."

NAZIMOVA (*film actress*)

"Certainly she was one of the greatest divas that ever graced the silver screen! Known for her personal drive and sense of the outré, Nazimova was a force to be reckoned with, exacting, demanding and, at times, rather caustic. But having said all that, she was a dream on the creative level and therein laid the challenge, the thrill of working with her. Our age difference was evident yet it faded in our scenes together, whenever we were in front of the camera. I strove to match her ferocity, though in a quieter way. Concurrently challenged in this production and taken with Natacha, I was distracted whenever I could be, always wanting to catch her eye.

Nazimova played off my interest in Natacha and I used it to respond to her character. Indeed, every time we had a close-up I summoned my attraction to Natacha to be a good Armand. Nazimova could be haughty and she was, at times, with me but there was an underlying respect, acknowledgment of my abilities. We really worked hard together and mostly I am satisfied with the results.

Madame's brand of exoticism, unfortunately for her, began to wane following this outing." (*re: "Camille" ~ Paramount, 1921.*)

CARMEL MYERS (*film actress*)

"Imagine my delight when I discovered Universal was going to use me as a leading man, and with Carmel, who had a following I hoped would take me along with her, blazing the fame trail. Well, it did not quite work out that way.

We really had fun with each other making those films. (*"All Night" and "A Society Sensation."*) But let's face it, the scripts were banal and production values relatively low, B pictures or maybe even C though we did provoke a few smiles with our pratfalls and the outlandish nature of the plots.

Carmel was easy on the eyes and game for whatever, to give it a go. I fancied her, at least mentally, but my attention was of the puppy dog variety, brief attraction with little or no heft. A purple ruffled dress, that is my memory of her as I conjure up our films, how last I saw her during the shoots, or rather how I wanted to see her, in my off-camera role as a pretender."

WANDA HAWLEY (*film actress*)

"I have referenced her before in these writings, re: "*The Young Rajah.*" She was a bit haughty, and not unlike her character in the sense that she resisted what she knew not of. No, I would not call her open. And she was recalcitrant about this role, complained at times too, whereas I gave it what I could. We were able to pull off our characterizations in the scenes we shared, make audiences believe there was attraction, allure. But for me there was none.

A disjointed shoot and a director who was diffused at best in his approach to the material, these were just some of the factors that caused me to reconsider my relationship with Paramount. Even so, I am proud of this picture today, what it attempted to portray: shed light on the insidiousness of prejudice and expound upon grander themes, intuitive abilities being one of them."

DOROTHY DALTON (*film actress*)

"She was not the first choice for her role in the picture we did together ("*Moran of the Lady Letty*") yet she was altogether perfect as it turned out, for she could portray an ambiguity about love and embrace the spirit of adventure at the same time. Interestingly, one of the leading ladies I most enjoyed working with. There was no personal relationship per se but when we were on set, submerged in our roles, there was an ease present, a sense of knowing what to do and say that would be commensurate with our characters, so nothing artificial, no trying too hard. We fit the mold the script had defined.

I did not work with Dorothy again but she did leave an impression, and she was a better actress than many gave her credit for. An exhilarating shoot that one, maybe a stretch of credulity ~ **oui, un peu**, (*yes, a little*) but with a dash of swashbuckler, on both our parts, and slightly intense also. Great rapport is how I would summarize our interaction."

(Rudy with Vilma Banky in "Son of the Sheik.")

(Rex Ingram sharing his ideas with Rudy on the set of "The Four Horsemen of the Apocalypse" ~ Metro, 1921)

COLLEAGUES

REX INGRAM (*directed Rudy twice, at Metro Pictures*)

"Two peacocks loathe to groom one another; this was the essence of my interaction with Rex. He could have been an actor, as well as a director, throughout his career ~ so multi-talented was he. In directing me, he wanted **parco** (*sparing*) instead of passionate, wanted me to be dryer in "*The Conquering Power*" ~ a bit more of a twit too, the spoiled boy who has to try harder to adapt. But I saw the part as I saw it, and though he thought I tried to upstage his wife, I did not, which you, the viewer, will agree upon screening the results. Rex imagined what was not. Alice and I had excellent rapport but we were not physically attracted to each other.

There was also a smidgen of resentment on both our parts. He felt he should have received more praise for "*The Four Horsemen of the Apocalypse*" and I thought he was trying to crimp my style, turn down my voltage on our second outing. Karmic disturbances that now have been adjusted and regulated. Mere bagatelles, there is nothing much of consequence to report about our very minor tugs of war!"

CHARLIE CHAPLIN (*film actor and along with Douglas Fairbanks, Mary Pickford, and D.W. Griffith, one of the founders of United Artists Pictures*)

"Although he was somewhat of an enigma, I found him rather brilliant, engaging, and conversant on any number of subjects. He was also quite eclectic in his personal tastes and very sure of himself professionally. We did socialize upon occasion but never approached the border of intimate friends, the kind who would share most things.

During *"The Eagle"* shoot, he did appear several times to reassure me, and the cast, I suppose to marvel at our accomplishments, be the goodwill ambassador for United Artists Pictures. He knew our work would please the public, had a smell for that kind of thing.

I did not witness any of the quirks that have been assigned to Mr. Chaplin over the years, nor did I ever observe him in character as the little tramp, even though hints were there, present in the way he moved ~ body language you say today. I remain grateful for the opportunity he, Doug, and Mary gave me: to become a part of their film family."

GRETA GARBO (*film actress*)

"It is not common knowledge that she and I ever had a face to face. It occurred one night, shortly after her arrival in Hollywood, when we were introduced at a rather chic dinner party with only a few guests. I found her alluring, sphinx-like, yet there bubbled a joy inside, an effervescence that pulled one in. An old soul she was, with an eye that could spy, meaning she saw into the depths of any interaction. How could she be an outstanding actress were this not so? Yes, Miss Garbo, for that is how I addressed her, as did our hosts. Tuxes and tails, jewels and gowns, it was one of those glamorous evenings in Los Angeles towns.

We took note of each other, in so many words, and liked what we saw. We did not meet again, however. An acknowledgment, therefore ~ respect exchanged in the flit of a glance."

DOUGLAS FAIRBANKS (*film actor, employer, friend*)

"Mr. Hollywood! If ever there was a quintessential figure, someone audiences could rally around as both hero and rogue, it was Doug. He had the magic, the one that propelled him to great heights. Of course, that he had control over his pictures was paramount. He did not need to kowtow to studio demands or act in simpering productions, stale pieces of bread, even crusts, which is what I would liken some of the product of those days to be. And Doug was a really nice guy, funny, witty, always with a sly sense of humor. His physical prowess obviously delighted viewers, made him, for a while, top box office. And he picked his projects well, wished me all the best with "*The Eagle*" and "*Son of the Sheik*" once I had joined the United Artists stable of stars.

We were a bit competitive physically, had to show off to each other once in a while, our abilities with riding and sports. I have fond memories of Doug, and how our careers were, in a way, complimentary. My favorite Fairbanks film was "*The Thief of Baghdad*." An incredibly impressive work of art and it was fun to watch!"

MARY PICKFORD (*film actress, employer, friend*)

"Mary, Mary! One of the sweetest women I knew in those days, even though she had a spine of steel! She would need one, given the enormous number of starring roles she had, making pictures non-stop. A strong acumen she possessed and she knew how to 'niche' herself, choose roles that became her. She displayed a bit of mothering where I was concerned, and in truth I found that delightful, sublimely charming. Mary was a superb hostess and I was fêted by she and Doug on numerous occasions. We were, I suppose, the royalty of the day, at least in a slightly dusty town named Hollywood.

I did know Doug a bit better as Mary had an aloof angle she displayed when anyone crossed a certain line. This does not mean there were any negatives between us, just societal convention, a business, collegial relationship there, in addition to being friends. What glamour she exuded in person, which ordinarily did not comport with her screen characters! Just goes to show you how gifted she was as an actress. Exuberance: Mary, Doug, and I engendered that in each other. It was the primary descriptor of all our interactions."

PAULINE FREDERICK (*film actress, friend*)

"A society gal with show biz in her blood which, by the way, also had a touch of blue in it! Pauline presented herself very regally. Yet everyone loved her demeanor as she was not haughty in her elegance, her sense of persuasion, for persuaded one she did. And, such a lively ally! This is the essence of our interaction as there was no physical connection. Even so, we probably had sex in our minds now that I recall our energetic premise. How we intertwined ethereally! Pauline provided me with introductions and I see her now in my mind's eye, carrying a feather fan. Only she could pull that off!

We did not do any pictures together but I would have liked to have worked with her. She and I had evidentiary allure, noticeable palpitations that might have been of use when submerged in roles. Love to you, Pauline!"

JOHN BARRYMORE (*film actor*)

"A noble name, and man, who I thought worthy of the first, and only, Valentino award for an outstanding performance in a motion picture. His was "*Beau Brummel*" which I found sublime. We did not really know each other on the friendship level yet there was great respect and rapport professionally, in that arena. John was quite touched to receive my award, as it occurred prior to the establishment of the Academy. Perhaps I was being prophetic but Mr. Barrymore deserved to win a prize, so shapely were his characterizations. This film was a good excuse to comply. And, as it turned out, he was not formally recognized for any of his subsequent performances.

We did ride together a couple of times in the Hollywood Hills, and he was a dinner guest once at Falcon Lair. What a gifted body of work, his! And the nose, that famous profile, we could have had a contest about that! Oh yes, I met his brother and sister too, though far more superficially."

JOHN GILBERT (*film actor*)

"We were mirrors placed at the opposite ends of the same room, reflecting endlessly in the glass the illustrious proportions of our respective talents. John and I were each quite unique yet we both illumined the place, added some wattage to the proceedings, for very different reasons of course. He was a little surly which attracted the ladies while I was the one they might dream to conspire with, the savior in the sense that I was seen as an outlet or solution. John was more the catalyst, the man who swept in and changed his leading lady forever, also at times a bit of a lout which I was not in the least. Bad boy versus rascal, as it was my job to exude fun while he was more serious.

Box office buddies, our careers overlapped ~ his more ascendant perhaps at the time, mine more everlasting. We did meet, of course, at any number of parties and were always cordial. However, we were never friends per se, never did share anything of import. Another person with whom I could have had a profile contest and perhaps we did, at least in the minds of our audiences!"

CECIL B. DeMILLE (*director*)

"In Mr. Valentino's death we have lost a great artist. But fortunately we can look on death as progress and not as the finish." ~ C.B. DeMille

"One of the greatest seers of all time! What people do not know or at least not consciously so is that Mr. DeMille could read the public pulse better than most anyone in Hollywood. Not even the studio execs had a better nose for what would sell. And then he was brilliant in the execution, making loads of cash for Paramount along the way. He tweaked American sensibility, soothed it yet also was quite challenging, holding up a mirror so that we could look at ourselves. What a pioneer! What a student of morality! The mores of the 1920's were never clearer than in productions that flourished under his hand. Then too, the studio knew every DeMille picture was going to contain a certain amount of moxie. A man totally in tune with his times, he adapted, also did excellent work in the sound era, having a lengthy and laudable career.

We only superficially crossed paths but I observed him on his sets, saw how he challenged his actors, and worked with their occasional insufferableness too ~ truly a gifted individual!"

D.W. GRIFFITH (*director, employer*)

"I was smitten with his work upon first discovering it, fascinated as well. Mr. Griffith touched us on a very deep level, often hitting nerves in the process. In fact, sometimes you could say he was more of a dentist than director, extracting essences instead of teeth. His vision had few parallels, and he imbued his actors with the freedom to improvise, call forth every tick, every grimace, each of which was always pregnant with meaning. D.W. could be classified as a genius, such was his mien. And I, Rodolfo, one of his fans, was most appreciative of his originality, the way he developed his stories which invited audiences both to enter and participate in them

I did make his acquaintance and had the opportunity to converse about his approach to film-making. We spoke at length one night after I had become a United Artists

47

employee. Reserved, he, yet the scent of humanity was always on his breath, oozing out of every pore. He reflected the times, those 15 or so years when he reigned ~ perhaps even besting DeMille as a name to be reckoned with. Many thought D.W. a giant of a man and I am not referring to his stature. One of my Griffith favorites was *"Way Down East"* ~ Miss Gish in all her brilliance married to a compelling scenario, beautifully realized."

MARION DAVIES (*film actress, friend*)

"Marion and I had chemistry. By this I mean we were great friends, even though our contact was infrequent. I admired her sparkle, her comedic chops, which translated to everyday life. Light-hearted and fearless in whatever role, she was game for any sort of pratfall or sidebar. Sideways glances too, the kind audiences found delightful! She chose a challenging pathway, canoodling with whom she did, a bird in a gilded cage. But she made more of that cage than any other woman in show business who might have found herself in similar circumstances. She loved to dance, kibitz at parties, share her joy, which she also did on screen. Audiences did not really know, not fully anyway, who backed her career but that, in the final analysis, mattered not. Marion had talent and she displayed it in every vehicle, even those costume-driven ones!

How I delighted in engaging with her and she called me 'Rudykins' to tease, cause me to smile, which it did, every time. Love to you, Marion. We have had a chat or two on this side, mostly for old time's sake. She and I have crossed paths on numerous occasions but in a friendly fashion only."

ERICH VON STROHEIM (*director, actor*)

"One of Hollywood's most notable personalities, he traded on his German ancestry. We met, of course, although casually, on several occasions and I was very familiar with his work, his explorations of some of mankind's baser instincts, and with such visual cues so as to sear them into the minds of those who watched his productions. He possessed great creativity which mostly flowed freely though he would self-block from time to time, leading to cost overruns and friction with studio heads, or accounting departments.

A von Stroheim film I fondly remember is "*Foolish Wives*" where he was also on screen. He did not achieve the pinnacles others did as far as consistent popularity and box office but his films sparked controversy and therefore were the subject of many discussions. His Prussian bearing was slightly affected yet no one questioned it ~ part of his allure, the attraction that was von Stroheim. He and I did not have a strong connection but I admired his ability to be daring, stretch limits, call attention to some of the issues of the day."

ADOLF ZUKOR (*CEO of Famous Players-Lasky/Paramount Pictures, employer*)

"Delusions of grandeur which were contrasted with his height, something he was always sensitive about. I had few direct interactions with him yet he was a powerbroker, and in my case, very catalytic for my career, more so than I realized at the time. His mind was like a steel trap in that he carried Paramount's production schedule with him, had it committed to memory. He was partial to Miss Swanson, above all, because she made him so much money. Artistic license was given lip service during his reign but it was the dollar who ruled the lot. That said, I am grateful Paramount moved me along, furthered my career, again in completely unexpected ways: the début of the Sheik, he who captured the imagination of America!"

WILLIAM CAMERON MENZIES (*art director, production designer*)

"Possessed of great ingenuity and vision, he was one of the most important contributors to the film confection I became involved with, "*Cobra.*" His work was already legendary prior to that shoot so it was a coup for him to work with us, namely Ritz-Carlton and Paramount. I spoke with him frequently, shared my opinions, which he welcomed. He was a collaborator, not a dictator, when it came to set design and he liked input. We were aesthetic buddies, enamored with sharing our creative eye. Later we worked together again on "*Son of the Sheik*" where he also conceived of and then shepherded the set decoration, very ably, I might add."

GILBERT ROLAND (*film actor, acquaintance*)

"As a young man he attended a party where I was present. He had just completed filming "*The Plastic Age*" and was squiring a starlet, someone whose name was more on people's lips at the time. But Gilbert caught the eye of both sexes. At one point in the evening, he approached me to speak of some of the roles I embodied, lo, to ask my advice which I freely gave. He was an admirer of my work in "*Camille*" which, as it turned out, was a part he played later in a re-make, very successfully I might add. I was impressed with his sincerity, also the lucidity with which he spoke. And I note he had a long and illustrious career!

We had previously met, albeit only briefly, on the set of "*Blood and Sand*" where his father, a former bullfighter, had been my trainer. It was Gilbert who helped me navigate the suit of lights, my costume for the arena."

GEORGE FITZMAURICE (*director of "Son of the Sheik"*)

"The captain at the helm; he whose expertise was choice. No one, I believe, could have handled that material with more verve and sensitivity, simultaneously. And remember he had to be all over the map in terms of dealing with actors and their wildly varying styles and characterizations. I am delighted to have worked with George; he was the perfect choice for my final film, the one incidentally I am probably most remembered for today, and the one most often shown at festivals or one-offs of silent films.

George had a highly developed intuition which he ably used to highlight various aspects of the scenario or plot. Many flashes of insight! And you could see his mind ticking like a clock, putting them all in order. I salute your work, **Signor**; **grazie mille**!" (*Many thanks!*)

LON CHANEY (*film actor, acquaintance*)

"We brushed elbows on numerous occasions and I did make it a point to attend the premier of "*The Phantom of the Opera*" on account of Norman (*Norman Kerry*) as it was one of his most prestigious pictures to date.

Probably no one in Hollywood played with the underbelly of reality more than Lon. Even so, he had an ebullient side, could actually be funny ~ his humor so ripe and rife, what no one would really believe but it's true! Indeed, he often

51

joked when cloaked in some monstrous face or costume. Being a ghoul was his cup of tea but he did not take it seriously, saw these characters as simply a means to express his art, flickers on the silver screen.

Lon was proud to be a father and spoke to me of his son's progress, whatever the endeavor might have been. Good friends, no, but we gravitated, were happy to seek each other out at parties and events. And I could always expect him to be cogent, no matter what libations flowed. A good man, Mr. Chaney!

First at Universal and then MGM, he attacked each part head-on, using his creativity to develop a look and gait that were completely commensurate. And he was fearless in his portrayals, with audiences caught somewhere between staring at the screen and averting their eyes."

JOSEF VON STERNBERG (*director*)

"This was a man whose genius was palpable. Indeed, when you were around him it wafted through the air. He had a visual love affair with Marlene Dietrich, of course, but that occurred later, years after we met. There was a playful aspect to him, one you would not expect given the rectitude of his Teutonic background. And, he had one of the most trained eyes in the world of cinema, could arrange any set and photograph it, to maximum effect. A savant of sorts and, more importantly, a mensch!"

COLLEEN MOORE (*film actress*)

"Colleen and I once flirted innocently at a grand reception, with champagne pouring, raining even. She looked glorious, just as you see her on screen. A tenuous connection, however I will say that Colleen has returned to the flesh and is a current actress, on her way up in terms of notoriety and career. She, in this capacity, has availed herself of my support on more than one occasion, that is to say we have a mutual agreement, at the moment, for me to act as one of her guides.

Just as fresh and vivacious now as she was then!"

(*Rudy as a Native American warrior*
~ homage to Black Feather)

MENTORS

A*lthough everyone Rudy ever met was in some sense a mentor, as was he to them, there are only two, besides his mother, that really stand out: Black Feather and Meselope.*

"I do want to pay homage to my spirit guides; they all were, and are, wonderful companions, delightful as a matter of fact!"

BLACK FEATHER (*Native American spirit guide*)

"Black Feather was the type who would tap me on the shoulder prior to any important life decision, as if to say "Rudy, is this really what you want to do?" He was a validator, therefore, of last resorts. Not him per se, but his imploring me to reflect placed me exactly where I should be: on the hot seat as emperor of my own domain for we are our only final arbiters, in all cases. Black Feather's presence in my life also injected instinct, a most important element of Native American lifestyle, what their survival often depended on. So I followed mine, and was encouraged to by him, in direct communication and not, within and without.

He was a mentor par excellence **et je suis fort reconnaissant du rôle qu'il a joué,** (*and I am very grateful for the role he played*) often center stage. **Merci, mille fois!** (*A thousand thanks!*) We work together now which you should not be surprised to hear, as comrades and compatriots. Love, Rodolfo."

MESELOPE (*Ancient Egyptian spirit guide*)

"A different story, as he and I did know each other once in incarnated life whereas that is not the case with Black Feather. Meselope was a scholar who advised me, a sounding board in the position I held under Pharaoh Horemheb, that of Vizier, the one you (*speaking to the author*) are also familiar with, where we sometimes walked the halls at night seeking shooting stars. Later he moved up the ranks to keeper of my scrolls, master scribe, overseeing others. So that life-time left a strong imprint on my soul and I carried the energy inside and, as I expressed Rudy, some of it appeared. Meselope knows how to anchor. That is how he helped Natacha and I when we called out to spirits to respond to our questions, held automatic writing sessions to create our book. (*"Day Dreams," published in 1923.*) He, too, is a trusted comrade.

Meselope carries the scent of ancient Egypt, incense, perfume, and along with that, the consciousness, great order and purpose of that society. For me, in that incarnation, it was truly a wonderful place to be alive. Oddly, he has an even stronger connection with Natacha having once been her father and then again her prince. His was an exemplary role in each of our lives. I remain eternally grateful to him and here we do also converse. What a solid, constructive force in the Universe, this is Meselope!"

RELATIONSHIPS & SIGNIFICANT OTHERS

T *here has always been a great deal of interest in Rudy's relationship with his second wife, Natacha Rambova. Was it a sham? Did they really love each other? How did they get along? She was, undoubtedly, one of the most significant individuals he ever met.*

NATACHA RAMBOVA (*second wife, creative partner, soul mate, friend*)

"Madame Valentino, the name some sarcastically applied, was a terrible misnomer. Natacha, for all of her magnificent presence and experience as a dancer, was actually rather shy and appeared to be distant, removed as a result. But, she was hardly that. In a one-on-one or in small groups her spark was divine. Shall we say she was a natural empath and was always imparting very cogent impressions and random bits of wisdom, never unwanted, I might add, or things that were intrusive, but rather oh so appropriate for the moment. As tough as she seemed, however, there was a fragility about her and a sense, on my part, that she needed to be held, and often.

Natacha was a soul mate, and we went deep in our understandings of each other and the world around us. Also, I liked her style, found it terribly appealing, as she was not much like other women in the sense that she forever applied her creative eye to wherever she was and whatever she was doing. **Petits éclairs**, (*little flashes of light*) these are what emanated from her being on a moment to moment basis. And we often had a laugh or two in the bedroom, when we were purely ourselves, without **pudor** (*shyness*) or pretense. A symphony it was, for most of our 'time.'

I hate that she is often so reviled, when she did not merit anyone's **méprise**. (*Scorn.*) Were there hard edges? Of course, and I, too, had my own!

This is a woman who was trendsetting in everything she did and her take on style was uniquely her own, the long hair, braids, 'hatteries' ~ meaning she had a slew of chapeaux to choose from and chose them she did, as she would a crown. Her look was always alabaster, a bit pale, but this is what I, in particular, found attractive, purely on the visceral level. She offered me contrast, was complimentary too, which is why you see us so poised in all our extant photos. We felt extremely 'golden' as a couple, our inner lights able to shine forth as we charged them for each other, which you could liken to electric storage batteries that were eternally in reception, naturally reactive. Yes, we had a dynamic that was worth noting, a mutual magnetism. How many hours we spent discussing aspects of the film industry, our respective careers and talents which, as you the reader will note, dovetailed quite nicely. Stimulating it was to be in Natacha's presence, to imbibe of her imposing fund of knowledge which was always on display, **étalé comme dans un grand magasin**. (*Arrayed, like in a department store.*)

Natacha was enthralled with blending various modalities, not only in her work life but also personal. She did not want our union to be commonplace and at times I really had to stretch myself, acclimate (as I was encumbered with Italian/European mores) in order to see where she was, what she wanted, when she wanted ~ to be a true companion. We were frequently quite lusty and used the dynamics of our sexual encounters to enhance, as well as define, our artistic natures. Opposites attract and we certainly were living examples of that premise!

You wonder, dear friends, what fascination she held for me, why I was so taken with her? Alluring, Natacha was a siren, (also in a sense Sisyphus) calling out to sailors, if I may invoke those images in your collective memories. But no monster she, nothing like her detractors made her out to be. Aloof, perhaps, even at times with me, yet inside there bubbled cool passion, grit, and an overriding spirit of adventure. Yes, this was the biggest draw! Every day with Natacha, in her company, felt like an adventure, and we were co-conspirators in that quest, whatever it was, whether to popularize a 'look' or present our case, such as the desire to produce more quality products, the dispute I had with Paramount Pictures, my employer during the greater part of our relationship.

Now many questions arise and I intend to deal with them, though perhaps not the most intimate. Did Natacha remain faithful, and did I remain faithful to her? This topic has been the subject of much speculation. We were faithful on the soul/spiritual level, committed, and primarily physically though we each had minor lapses on the latter front. Neither thought it odd or out of bounds, however, as one of our mutual agreements was never to stifle the other, never to

59

interfere with the other's learning experiences. So, none of these indiscretions had a deleterious effect on our interactions. In fact, sometimes they enhanced them. We were unconventional for the time and even in this modern day in many communities we would be considered as deviating from the norm. The who matters not; neither does the what. That we sampled life was of primary importance. Now I see these choices as having been instrumental in our mutual growth and development, as important as our professional decisions for which we became rather widely known, especially given the fascination of the press for our every move. In that life-time, in Natacha's company, I have never felt more comfortable and if you could speak with her through the either, in the same way as you are with me, I think she would concur.

Again, her sense of fashion was impeccable, the wave or cutting edge of what was to be always in the forefront of her consciousness. Natacha on the bow of the ship, sometimes steering it too! I did not want a shrinking violet and my wish was granted. But no soft touch either was I, two respective and respectful souls in a rather well-balanced partnership. Now you know the truth!"

Rudy, did you have a true love?

"Though not an intimate relationship, my mother was one and in her fashion, Natacha. And of course there were others too, glimmers I would call them rather than full-fledged loves, of all colors and stripes. Yes, like a multi-colored flag is love, any part of which is extremely rewarding. We all have some experience with true love while in the body. That is just one of the things we come to know more viscerally."

Are you and Natacha in contact now?

"We are not together per se in the Great Beyond. Our work has been completed. Actually, we finished what we had to as Rudy and Winifred, who she really was, as you know. We can communicate freely in the Astral, as desired, but we do not gravitate. I would liken it to old friends/flames who keep in touch from time to time. That said, we have tender spots for each other. She communicates with some in the flesh also, mostly around the arts and creativity. Muse-like she is and still with a preponderance of female energy."

BLANCA DE SAULLES (*love interest, sexual partner*)

"I had feelings for her: a young man's passion, an unattainable woman, someone who could teach me a thing or two. We tangoed in a sexual way but did not mate in the true sense because we were not soul-compatible. But we did dabble in sensuality, on the dance floor and off. She tickled my fancy, that's all. Taught me about **le haut monde** too." (*High society.*)

JEAN ACKER (*first wife, friend*)

"She was a pal more than anything else, like the character 'Moran' I would say (*making reference to one of his films, "Moran of the Lady Letty"*) ~ someone to do things with while commiserating on the vagaries of life. Not a soul mate but a gift, nonetheless. Embarrassing it was to marry without a wedding night but she did spark me to delve into my own psyche as a result, to reflect on what I really wanted. We reconnected, as you know, later in life. A good person though in that life-time her personality was somewhat obtuse.

I admired her raw interior, unformed as it was to a certain extent, a blank slate that I, in a prideful way, thought I could imprint. Little did I know of her predilections which she kept under wraps rather effectively. So the ingénue I perceived was far more schooled in the ways of the world than I would have ever guessed. That is why I did not see it coming, her skittishness which translated to a decision to make herself unavailable, **sans mots**. (*Without explanation.*) It was left to me to figure out which eventually I did.

This is not to say that Jean was duplicitous. But she most certainly was not fully in touch with her true desires when she dallied with me, entertaining the idea of 'Mrs. Valentino.' I am glad we transcended those events and buried the hatchet, smoked a peace pipe together. And yes, I do use that analogy very consciously as she and I are connected in the Native American spiritual realm. Appearances can be deceiving!"

POLA NEGRI (*film actress, lover, friend*)

"Pola/NOLA. She was like the city of New Orleans, an endless **fête**, (*celebration*) always ready for a lark. Restless she was and high-strung but very secure in herself and adept at creating an image. She helped me burnish mine, to cement my place in the pantheon of lovers. She doted on me to a certain extent and I basked in the attention, a much different dynamic than I had with Natacha, who was more cerebral and reserved.

Pola mostly realized the depths of my despair over the dissipation of my links to Natacha and she strove to fill in the blanks with great gaffes of gaiety. I say gaffes because sometimes she tried too hard whereas that was something she never needed to do. So we filled up our time with each other, proceeding down rose-strewn pathways, all the while knowing we were stand-ins for the 'real thing.' Playing at and with love is how I would define the essence of our relationship. Did we have fun doing that? Of course and Pola's ability to pack a punch on the energetic level was quite appealing. Her aura always glistened, christened as it was with raindrops and rainbows. Such was her charisma which accentuated my own. That is to say it was easy for us to play house, and lovers.

A cautionary tale, ours, for some of it was cardboard."

MARION BENDA (*Ziegfeld girl, lover, friend*)

"She was so effervescent I found being in her company like sipping a glass of champagne! We inspired the libertine in each other and ran with that as far as time and circumstances would allow. Many rough edges among the delights which, if I have any regrets, would be those. Her beauty was obvious; that was not even a consideration in the attraction. What was paramount instead was her heart, so fragile and fresh, so open to my own. Sacred and profane were our interactions, and intermittent at best.

What will surprise you is that sex produced a pregnancy, so it was she that might have provided me with an issue, not anyone else. The story has a dark aspect to it, one that I am not proud of, where I, through the urgings of my manager, acceded in putting my reputation and career first. So this, friends, is possibly the first time you will have heard of this happenstance.

About the progeny, there is little to tell. Unremarkable as this was not supposed to happen, not in my script, the overall metaphysical one, a slip-up. And suffice to say, no direct descendant of mine walks the earth today. Marion, her essence, who once again is in the flesh, and I continue to make amends. An on-going process but at least we can smile about it now. What I remember most about Marion is her grace in positioning herself, however she was planted, and did we ever imbibe, drink each other in!"

DAMIA (MARIE-LOUISE DAMIEN)
(singer, mentor, intimate)

"Yes, I met her and was rather taken, more with her fame than sexual allure although I must admit there was also that draw. She schooled me on the art of life, her bohemian ways, which I found beguiling. We played, and you can inject what you will, interpret that comment as you see fit!

Chanteuse de grand coeur, elle faisait allumer son ambiance, à chaque tour." (*A singer with a big heart, she lit up whatever space she occupied.*)

(Rudy and Natacha at their first wedding, in Mexico. Because his divorce from Jean Acker was still pending at the time, it unfortunately had to be annulled. RV and NR married again later during the Mineralava Tour, in Crown Point, Indiana.)

CAREER

SILENT FILM

"As an actor, it was my express purpose to make people think and silent pictures, devoid of language except for inter-titles and that which was primarily imagined, were wonderful vehicles for achieving that goal. Moreover, I was meant to be inspirational, to move audiences to a higher level of thinking. What you may perceive of as entertainment, therefore, may instead be considered a form of advanced education.

There's purity evident in silent film that is second to none. The elaborate ruses, the exceptional muses, the shortest of fuses, all these can be depicted with fierce intensity ~ to an even greater degree than in talkies. Fact is, the eye sometimes catches more than the ear. This is a premise that I can ascribe to, especially given my experience in the movie industry. The eyes tell it all, on screen and off. Again, a narrowing of the aperture, that is what watching a silent film affords, in a way very much like meditation. Indeed, most of our dreams are like silent movies. Nothing need be said in order for them to be salient.

Silence offers us an opportunity to focus. It narrows our attention spans, often making us more laser-like in our affectation. Lost we become in our eyes with the 'word' removed from the equation. Word, while powerful when combined with sight, is replaced in silent film with the phenomenon of music, a clearer and more definitive representation of vibration. The spoken word can divert sometimes, add complication ~ ambiguity, if you will, while the combination of a visual with music takes the viewer to a special place, dare I say to a context where the experience is heightened and therefore ingested, digested, and excreted into something new, all within the speed of the eye of a gnat."

RUDY ON RUDY

"I had the good fortune to be blessed with an expressive body and face. In fact, they were gifts and I used them well during my brief time in motion pictures to communicate my thoughts without the benefit of voice. What did I want to impart? The overall message was one of love ~ specifically that love overrides all other considerations and is the most powerful force in the Universe. This we all know, of course, on the cellular level, but our personalities need to be reminded of it time and time again. Not only that, it was my goal to present those who watched my films with alternatives, ways of being that they could then either accept or reject as they saw fit. Like all films, mine were instructive. That was their real reason for being."

Again, the context of silence is sometimes all the louder. With just a flick of the wrist or a slight movement of the eyes, I could communicate the essence of love, that state of being when we feel especially buoyed, supported beyond our wildest beliefs!"

WAYNE ON RUDY

My contention is that what critics had/have to say about Rudy's body of work and persona, either during the 1920's or now, is irrelevant. The proof is in the pudding, and Rudy is quite a good cook! Indeed, his films are still thought of as 'must-sees' for those who love silent films and his luster as an icon of love has not dimmed. In fact, I would say that of late it grows stronger, given the spate of Rudy-related books, rare photos, and new DVD releases that have come to light ~ especially during the past 10 years, and with more on the horizon.

That said, the people who have seen his films know the truth and, therefore, will not be influenced by anyone's jaundiced eye or attempt to be snarky. Rudy was a wonderfully nuanced actor, who fully owned every part he inhabited. For that is what he did in front of a camera, imbue them with soul! Did he ever go general in his roles? Sure, when the script and/or director called for it. But if you look carefully, there gems in each one, when his character projects incredible luminescence and touches everyone's heart.

Audiences always trump the critics. And Rudy continues to be one of the most talked-about and viewed stars of all time!

LATIN LOVERS

"My début in films ushered in a whole new era: what was what, a realignment of values and mores, also the standards of male essence, how that was projected. So, the Latin theme was inaugurated. I was the pioneer and then others, some of whom had only tentative connections, became known. I was Paramount's darling, Antonio Moreno, **un po'**, **anche lui** . (*A little, him too.*)

We were derided for our slickness yet worshiped from afar. Ah yes, careers were born by banking on this phenomenon, the exotic, the other, the slightly unpredictable swarthy lover as encapsulated, perhaps, by the screen persona of the Sheik. There were so many appellations, nicknames applied to us, some of which sound exceedingly silly now."

POSSESSIONS

R udy had an eye for beauty which was reflected in his innate good taste. An inveterate collector, he especially loved clothes, cars, and 'objets d'art.'

Can you comment on your famous slave bracelet?

"It remains in a collector's hands and, more specifically, it sees not the light of day, having its resting place now in a safe of some sort. The slave bracelet was a tangible token of the love between Natacha and me. I did not see it as a symbol of captivity and neither did she. It was simply an avant-garde concept, realized. Women wore a ring of betrothal, why not a bracelet for a man? It was Natacha's idea, and design, and I was more than happy to run with the thought, play it out in public."

Some have hypothesized that one of your rings was cursed. What say you about that suggestion?

"A story and nothing more than that! First of all, I did not believe in curses, contrary to what some biographers have implied, although I did have a cat's eye ring; that is true. I did not have bad luck, however, not any that I considered as such and certainly none I would attach to that ring. This is a fable that has gotten more elaborate over the years!"

Your 1923 Avions Voisin is currently on display at the Nethercutt Museum in Sylmar, CA. Any comments?

"One of my most prized possessions, ever, **cette voiture-là!** (*That car!*) A marvel of technology and speed, it was customized especially for me. Wind in my hair, and sails, when I drove that car; what freedom, what bliss! If I could have lived in it during the first week it was mine I would have gladly done so. Like a new jewel, you could not stop staring at it ~ polish and spit, not a speck of dirt or grime!"

Can you tell us why it was important for you to buy Falcon Lair? Did you see it as the ultimate possession?

"Not in the least! I would certainly have kept going, given half a chance! On Natacha's part there was great resistance, or rather she used the distance from Hollywood Blvd. to begin distancing herself in our relationship. Well, this house was more about me; I have to admit that my ego was a bit out of whack around this purchase. I saw it as natural progression. Natacha saw it as a sell-out. In her mind, Rudy was 'going Hollywood,' or more specifically, Beverly Hills. Therefore, she had no input in the design of the interior. It was a 'Rodolfo' show, **tour de force**. The orderly part of me surfaced at this time and I wanted space to display my collections, room to grow. What really sold the property, however, were the views. A huge bone of contention with Natacha, who really liked the house on Whitley Heights, this venture contributed greatly to the dissolution of our marriage. Nevertheless, it was written, that experience, something I just had to do, complete, as part of my script."

(*Falcon Lair, in all its glory!*)

(Rudy and Alice Terry in a scene from "The Four Horsemen of the Apocalypse" ~ Metro, 1921)

SKILLS &
ACCOMPLISHMENTS

T his is a list that could go on forever. If you will, allow me to mention just a few. In addition to actor: equestrian, author, metaphysician, spiritualist, dancer, cook, mechanic, boxer, and photographer. An incredibly talented individual!

"DAY DREAMS" (book of poems by Rudolph Valentino, published in 1923)

"Everyone has them, therefore, what an apt title we chose! I say we because Natacha had input on the scope and depth of this endeavor. We wanted it to be simple yet modern, but also traditional in the sense that the themes are eternal, endemic to mankind. We did indeed call upon the spirits, reach out to many of the great poets and writers of the Ages to see if they wanted to contribute. Some did, some did not. Then we played with the verses we received, tweaked them you would say now. Natacha was rather astute when it came to choosing which efforts to include. She also had an ear for pentameter so she was integral to this work. It was my hand, however, that penned *"Day Dreams"* ~ acted as scribe, was the writer in the sessions we had. No one else, by the way, was involved with these transmissions. Natacha and I sat together as opposed to other circles where we were joined by June (*Mathis*) and some of her colleagues, primarily studio personnel.

The final product: we were proud of our accomplishment, what we had achieved. Indeed, a lovely collection resulted and I do believe the content continues to inspire consideration, pondering ~ to this day. No grand work of art, this book, but rather a quiet reflection on some of life's most frequently reoccurring elements and themes."

"HOW TO STAY FIT" (*health and exercise booklet by Rudolph Valentino, published in 1923*)

"The question of tone for me was answered in my daily activities which were always brisk and tinged with exertion. I wanted to share my views as I thought everyone needed to make an effort to try a little harder with their physical self, to push beyond their comfort zone. Rather straightforward, the contents, and I think just as apropos today as when originally written. This book appealed to the practical side of who I am and I saw it as a primer in self-preservation."

EXPERIENCES

"Experience is the mother's milk of any incarnation so I do want to isolate a few of mine."

Prior to moving to the United States, Rudy decided to explore Paris.

"One of the most remarkable experiences in my life had to do with my teenage adventures in France, Paris to be specific. The city of light shown in all of its splendors and I have fond memories, especially, of the first time I stepped foot there ~ ébloui I was, (*dazzled*) by its glamour and panache ~ the center of the world, not just for the French but for all Europeans. That my mother allowed me, even encouraged me to go, was rather amazing. She saw the visit as finishing school, an opportunity for me to polish my presentation in the world. I, on the other hand, saw it as an adventure, a chance to explore the demi-monde, the world of nightclubs and debauchery. Did I avail myself? Not overly so but I certainly stuck my toe into the water and sampled what Paris had to offer. Such lovely memories! Trysts, but more than that, as exciting as they were, the endless stimulations, the ideas, the poses, the many roses, one would say in almost every lapel, and the crispness of every foray, the mini-dramas ~ the countless millions that happened, it seemed, on street corners each night.

The time I spent in Paris, city of dreams, was perhaps my ultimate learning experience, what best prepared me for what was to come, in Hollywood, as well as my personal life ~ the attitude of **flâneur, bon vivant.** (*Pursuer of indolence and beauty.*) Love, Rodolfo…"

In December of 1913, Rudy sailed from Europe to New York on the SS Cleveland.

"What an American name, the former President, I believe, which I duly noted when it became clear that it was upon that ship fate had bestowed me to book passage. A sense of excitement, adventure, gripped me once I had the ticket in hand, a sense that destiny was going to be served on this journey, which it was! An opportunity to immerse myself in roles: the boy, the count, though faux he was. These characterizations, the ones I adopted onboard, served me well in later years as cameras rolled in any number of productions. Appearances, I toyed on this journey with the power of presentation, passed myself off as more than I was which did involve mingling with the most prestigious folks aboard, or at least who I thought them to be. The days, and nights, were spent lightly with plenty of spirits and a few card games, also deck promenades ~ **la passegiata, come abbiamo fatto in Italia.** (*Strolling, like we did in Italy.*) I met and bedded a couple of ladies, mere caprices in this case, for all of us. No one took it seriously. Meanwhile in the pit of my stomach was that sense of excitement, knowing that my future was at play, also a bit of apprehension as I never did want to seem like a greenhorn. So, the night we arrived in New York: one of the most magical of my life! Cold, snow, the phases of the moon, these are indelible memories forever etched upon the annals of my consciousness.

Upon disembarking I knew I had come home, found my place in the world ~ not that Italy wasn't also. It was just that America held far more fecund possibilities, lurking everywhere, and me ready to pluck them, like fruit from a tree."

After trying his hand at other kinds of work, Rudy decided to focus on dancing as a way to earn money, first in New York and later in Los Angeles, while also occasionally working as an extra in films. As time went on, he garnered a certain amount of fame by partnering in exhibition dancing. Here he makes reference to his early days in the United States, the nightclubs and thé-dansants (tea dances) he frequented as a paid employee.

"**La danse**: never a more freeing thing could there be, an opportunity for each sinew, each muscle, to perform, to be engaged, producing a whole set of movements, gliding across the floor, as a single person or in the company of others with whom you exchange energies, harmonics, rhythms. Couple dancing, especially, creates a grand synchronicity!

Thinking about it now makes me slightly dizzy, just a little bit giddy too! So dancing was certainly something I liked to do, in spades! Now could I earn a living with it? In my case, I was just good enough, not a master, but good, which enabled me to be gainfully employed and, at times, also receive the monetary attention of women who thought that tipping was expected. Did I ever seduce on the dance floor? Upon occasion, but mostly it was about providing an outlet, physical pleasure, to my partner that did not involve coitus. How many grand dames did I encounter, along with bored young ladies? It was quite a study in personality which proved helpful in the acting business. Also, the dance poses, the ones that were most often adopted in those days, provided me with the rectitude I needed, the stage presence that eventually was to translate to work as an actor.

I am grateful for my abilities with dance, as well as the opening of consciousness that always ensues. Think of it as a moving meditation. Dancing was something suited to my talents and I took advantage of it, was proud to be seen as accomplished!"

Rudy shared a 2 room, 2 bath suite at the Alexandria Hotel with friend and fellow actor Norman Kerry when he first arrived in Los Angeles in 1917.

"The buzz around this hotel preceded my arrival by a number of years. I was so excited, no, intoxicated, with the idea of living there that I was beside myself. For me it was the ultimate in those days, luxury that did not break the bank as we could actually afford it. My suite with Norman had many accoutrements, details that made it more replete, apt for those whose business it was to preen and then, hopefully, make people swoon every time they stepped outside their room. Living there I felt prepared to face the world. One of the happiest periods of my life, this sojourn in the hustle and bustle of downtown Los Angeles, and we belonged, were part of the movie industry!"

In 1921, Rudy and Natacha were unofficially living together in a rented house on Wedgewood Place in Hollywood which they later purchased.

"Natacha and I really got to play house when we lived on Whitley Heights. Both the architecture and setting were just unusual enough to appeal to our artistic natures, perhaps hers even more than mine as she had greater impact, a larger footprint, and more say about how that environment was formed and certainly, therefore, the final product. She often asked my opinion along the way, however, so I did not feel left out of this process. We wanted chic, also sleek, cozy too and I think we were able to blend all three.

I would be remiss if I did not say I loved living there, loved the views which of course reminded me of the ravine in Castellaneta, and also that home's proximity to the burgeoning neighborhood of Hollywood Boulevard, its cinemas and other venues. So we were accessible yet no one came knocking on our door, something that was not done in those days. Up on the hill, down in town, a perfect blend, that property, a wonderful set of ingredients to make a proper cake!"

Especially after Rudy gained box-office fame, he attended a plethora of parties.

"Oh how we loved costumes and indeed the hoi polloi of Hollywood were very addicted to looks so we often dressed up, covered our identities even more than when we were on screen. Gave us something to talk about, focus on. Now do not think I was bored in making this statement. Indeed, I learned so much from off the cuff remarks, things I overheard, and exchanges I had with my fellow actors. And in this milieu studio rivalries dissolved. We were equal, though often dressed outlandishly.

Here is where I exercised my propensity to want to sing when people gathered around the piano. Who knew? Oh I was a silent opera star wannabe!

Another facet of the party circuit was its reciprocity. We all shared in that at various times we were both hosts and guests. Hobnob is really the most relevant verb as I remember these events with fond regard."

Because of his contract dispute with Paramount Pictures following the shoot of "The Young Rajah," Rudy needed to generate some income so he and Natacha signed an agreement with the Mineralava Company to promote their beauty products. The Valentinos were a package deal and their part of the bargain was to travel around the United States and dance together, specifically the tango, at staged events.

"For me it was a terrific experience, and an opportunity for Natacha to share the spotlight. We often were exhausted, however, by the schedule which could require us to perform in a different city every night. Yet at the same time we were buoyed by the good will and, frankly, love that was exuded by our many fans. Natacha enjoyed polishing her dance skills and I welcomed the chance to dust off mine. We traveled in luxury, our own train car, and this closeness, actually, piqued our interest in each other. An expression of mutuality, the Mineralava Tour: Natacha not playing second fiddle! We were nurtured by it, as grueling as it was, beyond our wildest dreams. As I reflect now, am so grateful this occurred and, as you know, we tied the knot the second time around, near your old stomping grounds." (*re: Crown*

Point, Indiana, which is approximately 10 miles from where I was born.)

In 1923, Rudy returned to Italy for a visit. Here he speaks about his experiences in Rome.

"What a magical time in my life, savoring the delights of the capital I had not previously known, and fêted, upon occasion, in that pursuit. My task was to drink, figuratively **boire un coup** ~ taste the fruits of my renown and brush elbows with the movers and shakers of local and international film industry. I dreamed of doing a part in Europe, in Rome in particular, some Italian-based theme or project. Don't think it did not cross my mind! Well, the visit to Nero (*i.e. Emil Jannings on the set of "Quo Vadis"*) was a soul-awakening experience, to what my home country had to offer, on a deeper, more spiritual level, which I was ready to comprehend then and there, and which I had been unaware of, for the most part, during my youth in Castellaneta and Taranto.

How grand was Rome, how inspiring its monuments, history at every turn, under every block of pavement! Bravo! I listened and learned. This is what I did there: really saw, and really heard. In the sound of the crickets there is the murmur of the Senate and people of Rome, the roar of **Vox Populi**."

In 1926, Rudy purchased a Franklin Coupé to add to his stable of cars. Although of standard manufacture, it had a custom paint job, taupe, which was also the color of his 1923 Avions Voisin touring car and the carpeting in most of the rooms at Falcon Lair.

"Whenever I wanted to eschew my celebrity, I drove the Franklin, a vehicle whose relatively unassuming exterior belied a myriad of mechanical marvels, not the least of which was an air-cooled engine. American ingenuity at its best! And, I was a gear head in my spare time as I loved tinkering with cars and servicing them myself.

Shall we say there was a part of me that yearned to be a common man, someone with a relatively mundane job who would have aspired to drive a Franklin, an accountant perhaps? My joy with that vehicle resided in its operational ease, as well as trustworthiness. Franklins did not usually have breakdowns and their innards were tough. As you note, (*speaking to the author*) one of my favorite colors seemed to be taupe. **Eleganza**, (*elegance*) that is what that color bespoke. Errands, this and the Chevrolet were my errand cars, especially when I dabbled in **bricolage, fai-da-te**. (*Do-it-yourself projects.*) Was I ever lucky to have sampled a real cross section of engine-hood!"

Rudy was quite a fan of the great outdoors, spending time at the coast whenever he could.

"Going to the beach for me was like visiting a church. I saw God's handiwork in every grain of sand, every drop of water. I loved basking in the sun, baring my body, feeling breeze upon my skin. And any time I could go, to swim or walk, I would, as I always felt renewed, recharged. You remember my short film about a snooze on the beach? Oh friends, this, unabashedly, was one of my favorite things to do!

Swimming in the ocean was like being buoyed with love. At least that is how I saw it! And the beach is an egalitarian place, no movie stars there. We were all pared, taken down a peg by the glories of nature!"

For Rudy the Hudnut château on the French Riviera was the perfect setting, especially for what it contributed to the vibrancy of his relationship with Natacha.

"Some of my happiest days, ever, were at the Hudnut house in France, **chez mes beaux-parents.** (*At my in-laws.*) We were in our glory. Perfection reigned and my white summer suit, the one I often wore, was emblematic of a particular languor that was prevalent. We were all so relaxed and there is where I probably had the best chat, ever, with my brother Alberto.

Natacha, too, felt nurtured and was more vivacious in France, more in her element. Aspects of personality for both of us were slightly varied as compared to our lives in California and we welcomed the change, a true vacation from ourselves. They say geography plays a part, contributes to the flavor of self-expression. Well, the flavor of southern France was mighty tasty. Fond memories!"

In August of 1926, while on a publicity tour for "Son of the Sheik," Rudy fell sick and had to have surgery which, though successful, created unforeseen complications leading to his death.

"Usually my dying days are thought of in horror ~ 'why would that young actor who still had so much to contribute leave us so suddenly?' **Che brutto!** (*How ugly!*) Well my life, in that respect in particular, was exemplary as it reminded everyone that our time is finite. And do not think I was bereft; I was in pain, yes, but I saw the Light. And I had some days to ponder on my choices and relationships, to wonder what I might have done differently. This was a gift and although I thought I was not ready to depart, I was indeed.

In closing I also want to mention the extent to which I felt love coming to me while I was in the hospital, flowing in my direction, seemingly from all corners of the globe. **Beato me**!" (*Was I ever blessed*!)

PERSONAL QUESTIONS

1. What was your height?

"Five feet eight and a half inches ~ no more, no less!"

2. What were your color preferences?

"Smoky grays, muted golds, dark reds. And for flowers it was yellow, especially roses."

3. What was your favorite activity?

"There were many, of course. When not in the company of my fellow human beings it was anything that had to do with horses ~ such a noble and sensitive creature, one with whom I always had great rapport."

4. How would you describe your relationship with money?

"Like playing with a hot stove! I saw it as a commodity, something to use, for my own good, and that of others. Also, as a means to an end ~ in my case, numerous ends! Holding on too tightly to the reins did not run in my veins, in just about any life circumstance. So I pushed the limits when it came to finances, wanted to see how far I could go."

5. Did the aspersions cast by some newspapers on your masculinity contribute to your early demise?

"They had absolutely no bearing on it. The time, and manner, of death are calculated by the soul in question, something that is true for everyone. Was I annoyed, from an ego perspective? Miffed might be a better word because the hypothesis was so unfounded. It was obvious I presented in a male form and had fully embraced that status."

6. Did you have a favorite food?

"**No, mi piaceva mangiare quasi tutto.** (*No, I liked eating almost everything.*) But you could say seafood and, of course, pasta, with garlic and olive oil."

7. Following up, what say you about cooking? Did you have any aptitude in that arena?

"One of my greatest ambitions, ever, was to be a decent cook and I was more than that, I can assure you! Good taste was always a guest at my table, along with any number of friends. Did I cook a lot? No, but when I did gusto was the main ingredient. Simple dishes reminiscent of home, those are what I strove to prepare, especially **coi funghi.** (*With mushrooms.*) Yes, I also loved mushrooms!"

8. Did you have a favorite beverage?

"**Certo, il vino rosso!**" (*Of course, red wine!*)

9. In speaking about your films in this book, you referred to yourself as a 'clothes-horse.' What was your attitude towards clothing?

"I saw it as a means to express individuality, not as a modality of banality, way to fit in, and things had to be tight, meaning I wore nothing that did not become, did not love the contours of my body. You could say my style was **raffiné** (*refined*) and you would not be incorrect. And I also wanted to amaze, leave people in a daze, thrill them with cloth draped on a frame, for I was their picture!"

10. Did you have a favorite song?

"Yes, **E Lucevan le Stelle**, from "*Tosca*." I found the melody especially compelling."

11. What about music for dancing, any preferences?

"Think of those crank-up victrolas and their internal horns squeaking out music! But we loved to dance, and I, of course, favored tangos, any kind of music I could use to tango with, also quicker tempos for the two-step. I do not have a record title that I can cite, however, so this answer is, of needs, rather general."

12. Did you and Natacha discuss having children?

"Children and who did or did not want them, again, Natacha maligned! In theory, I wanted to be a dad, express love to the issues of my own flesh, and Natacha did think about it, very seriously, if she wanted to mother. But our careers intervened and we did not take that step. Natacha was never pregnant as some have speculated, more stories that were enflamed, sparks, embers ignited, many years later. The idea of father appealed to me more than mother did to her; that is so. But we were not sealed off, closed to that reality.

In the bigger picture, however, it was not our purpose, soul mission, for either of us, to be parents in that particular time sequence and that is why it did not happen. I suppose you could say our ideas were our children, and they were, indeed!"

13. Who were your favorite characters?

"Julio, of course, as well as Juan, followed by Ramón and Rodrigo, and let's not forget Vladimir! And then there's Ahmed, who I also very much liked but was not among my favorites."

14. How might you have fared in sound films?

"The 'talkies' would have reduced me to stereotype, to being another actor in a field of many, whereas silence provided me with the cloak of invisibility, meaning I could dive into a role and then easily wipe the slate clean after each performance. Voice, on the other hand, tends to linger, become imprinted upon the brain. So the visual was my calling and the source of my impact as an actor. Could I have acted in talking pictures? Of course and with a certain amount of panache but the mystery surrounding me would have been unveiled and its effect therefore diminished. And, my friends, this was not written in the stars, for me to make that particular transition!"

15. Who did you admire and why?

"Those I deemed to be brilliant, those who promoted the evolution of mankind, philosophically and practically. I was especially a fan of anyone who was able to expand the use of technology and gadgets! In terms of personality, one of my favorites was Houdini, for his showmanship and what I figured were his deeper waters. My colleagues were all somewhat emulative but there is no one except Marion Davies who stands out. I admired her ability to supersede her limitations, personal, and the ones she adopted to be able to enter the world of picture-making."

16. Why were you so enamored with your pets?

"I saw them as little people, the blessed beings that they are, though of different stripe and color. Yes, they have souls, which shine forth from their eyes and I loved them for that, the clear, cool, gazes we exchanged every time we appraised our respective positions. We always knew where the other stood, literally and figuratively."

17. Can you comment on your relationship with scent?

"For me, scent was an 'inspiring' agent. I felt more complete, stronger, when in that thrall and I chose several to be my favorites, to highlight certain aspects of my personality, what some would call the 'Rudy' persona. Know this: scent is a great mystifier as well as point of attraction. And it speaks to all the other senses, sometimes rather loudly. In that regard I especially remember liking *Maharadjah*."

18. How would you describe your fascination with jewelry?

"Wow, did I ever have a love affair with that concept – ornamentation! We, meaning men, once adorned ourselves so much more than during my Hollywood days. Indeed, in ancient times men strove to shine, and jewels, jewelry, were a means to that end. As Rudy, I wanted there to be that focus again so I collected multiple rings and watches, not too much else, with the exception of the famous platinum bracelet. Let's say that jewelry and gems are one of my callings. And like scent, they bespoke individuality, my brand, if you will."

19. What say you about your fans?

"They are those who make our efforts worthwhile, and I speak not only for myself but for everyone who perambulates in the world of entertainment, especially on the silver screen. My fans, in particular, have been and continue to be incredibly loyal, drawn to the Rudy persona for the source of it all, the divine spark that emanates, not only from my being, but from theirs – a celebration of such. What I am saying is that I act as a talisman for people to get in touch with themselves, their nether regions, meaning innards. Fans, I adore you! It is a mutual admiration society, them and me."

20. Were you aware of having health issues prior to August, 1926?

"Instinctively I knew there were problems, minor malfunctions in play, yet I attributed them to my life style which, in the final year, emphasized a dissolute bent. Lots of stimulation of all stripes and ilk, and loads of stomach cures, for that is where the distress was mostly felt, more acutely noticed. So yes, I had a clue but my consciousness was nonetheless astounded by the final turn of events, also the rapidity with which they occurred."

21. Can you comment on the phenomenon of people wanting to categorize you sexually?

"What a foolish enterprise! Why? Because each individual operates along a continuum, a fairly broad perspective of sexual behavior and predilections that are hardly definable and very fluid, ebbing and flowing depending on many variables which include time, place, manner of energy treatise and other cabooses, like appendages. So to categorize into neat little cubbyholes is almost impossible in this realm but nevertheless you can see patterns in each life-time, and that being said, I hope mine are clear, rather self-explanatory. Funny how much import people put on the issue of who is attracted to whom. Misplaced attention, I would say as there are many more important aspects to consider, the karmic wake, or trail, each person makes, for example."

22. How did being an expatriate impact your life?

"The issue of belonging ~ where did I fit? What, ultimately, did I claim and how did I claim it? My persona embraced the different, the unique, and I accessed all of my parts, all the nationalities I was associated with, to make that occur. Always aware I was not completely American, I wanted to be yet I remained a little apprehensive about turning my back on my roots, becoming too homogenized. So I was the expat, pure and simple, which added something to my allure, my image with the public, as actor and screen personality."

23. *Why the multiple visits to Palm Springs?*

"My love affair with that town had to do with differences, a habitat that was so unlike anything I had ever experienced before. And the land exuded laxity, a sense of the indolent. I found this soothing and on top of that I could play cowboy, something that was never to come to pass on screen. We were also protected there, very little press and no sense of being under a microscope. I loved the freedom and spontaneity I experienced in Palm Springs, also many intense conversations, with locals and show folk alike. Nature, too, shared her bounty, perhaps even more directly in that clime. The starkness appealed, and that is why we returned, repeatedly."

24. *Who was your favorite dance partner?*

"Joan Sawyer - a steely lady who was remarkably agile, quick in mind, spirit, and especially where the body was concerned. Her control over every muscle was a miracle to behold. And Joan was a free woman, master of her own destiny. All the men in her life were only there because she wanted them to be. Garnished was she, always knew exactly what to wear for which occasion. We relished our roles; I did not mind backing her up, for as a partner that is what I did. She was the star and I merely Signor Rodolfo. My, did we have a following! Even President Wilson knew of our acclaim!

Joan and I were friends, first and foremost. When we were on the road, we always did rehearse, the reason being to keep the performance fresh. In fact, sometimes we purposely changed the choreography just to shake things up. Not lovers, she and I, though we flirted with the idea. At least I did, and more than once! One of my highlights, the time I spent on stage with Joan. She shown and I was simply a reflector, gladly so."

25. Why did you pursue photography to the extent you did?

"For me the photographic camera was like a third eye. What I often discovered upon developing my films is that there was something in the frame that I had not actually seen, or not to its fullest glory, when I snapped the shot. What a revealing contraption! How I enjoyed taking photos, documenting lives, facial expressions, stances, scenery, ambiance, the whole package!

I had dreams of directing some day. That's why I sometimes watched DeMille or other directors, as well as paying full attention to the ones who were calling the shots on my own films. How grand! I have Paul Ivano to thank for his exquisite instruction in the art of the visual, in general, and in particular: how best to handle a camera. Love, Rodolfo."

26. Which films were you most impressed with and why?

"A film I admired was "*The Big Parade*" as it was a coda or so I saw it to "*The Four Horsemen*." Again, about the Great War and the insane futility of multiple killings, the karmic nature of it, but so beautifully portrayed, those characters, by Mr. Gilbert and Miss Adorée. A highlight in my movie-going experiences, and I was fond of many other pictures also, too numerous to mention. My perceived rival, Mr. Novarro, starred in a film that piqued my interest so I went to see it, attended the premier, as did I on many other occasions when films made their début. We had potboilers and fine art in movies; this is a dichotomy that has not changed. Upon reflection, I wish I had seen more of the product of the time but post-1921 I was busy with my own work.

Lovely visuals are what I remember most, how silence required us to think a lot more."

27. Can you comment on the concept of "la grande bellezza?"

"**Certo**. (*Of course!*) With either open or closed eyes we are continuously witnessing 'la grande bellezza.' (*Great beauty.*) Every breath brings further awareness of it, deeper understandings, for this phrase refers to what has been and continues to be wrought, the stuff of life: the mountain view, the river slough."

28. How did it feel to return to Castellaneta when you visited Italy in 1923?

"I felt elated, actually, to be able to walk those streets, see those buildings one more time and, of course, I was fêted, seen as a curiosity, the small town boy who made good in the world, also an exotic, a sophisticate who seemed to those he encountered as someone other than who he was. Not true, of course, but the term 'movie star' encourages projection, no pun intended! Happy to arrive and happy to leave, in the sense that I more fully understood why a life in

Italy would not have nurtured me to the extent that other options did. Bittersweet, therefore, sums up my interactions with the townsfolk of Castellaneta."

29. The volume of your possessions, as indicated by the auction catalogue of your estate, suggests that you had a propensity to collect. Can you confirm and if so how did that serve you?

"Yes, I did, but with a caveat: that each item I surrounded myself with be both imbued with beauty and an expression of my personal taste. Also, that it reflected something unique. So these were my motivating factors, as well as having been born under the sign of Taurus, a most tactile and sensually-oriented slice of the zodiac. Indeed, I loved the look and feel of things, period. True, I may have gone a bit overboard but it was done out of a love for beauty and the continual delight of finding specific manifestations, not because of any need to hoard or play the role of **avare**. (*Miser.*) Somehow I knew my time on Earth was going to be short and I wanted to enjoy it to the fullest. These baubles afforded me expanded consciousness and terrain upon which to luxuriate."

30. Why were you a proponent, and practitioner, of spiritualism?

"Everything is spiritual, and communication, thereof, is a natural phenomenon. Why was I a proponent? Because the study of it is so vast and I was intrigued with the possibilities. Of course, I was delighted with the insight that was always forthcoming. Also, the process seemed really easy to accomplish. Why not speak with your guides and on a regular basis too? This work, spiritualism, its practice, bound us together, Natacha and I, in quite a different matrix. We were Hollywood people, sure, but the interest represented our secret society. So we smiled and felt loved ~ what the practice provided. And it readied me to cross over, sooner than ever I would have expected."

31. How would you describe the role religion played in your life?

"The intricacies of religion, pomp and circumstance, pageantry, especially as they relate to the Catholic Church, were all incredibly appealing though I must admit I only gave lip service to some of the dogma. I saw my religion as a smorgasbord, to pick and choose from, which is not very different from most people. Beyond that, being associated with a religion provided a certain degree of comfort even though my spiritual tendencies and spiritualistic practices were not really supported and/or tolerated. I saw myself as a free thinker where religion was concerned which was my real salvation."

32. What can you say about your reputation as a daredevil behind the wheel?

"I was smitten with speed and often drove inappropriately for road, weather or traffic conditions. And, I had my share of accidents, tempting fate, some of which were never reported. Of course, when I wrapped the Isotta Fraschini around a telephone pole the press jumped all over that, picturing it as an escape from death, the lucky Mr. Valentino, rather than an exercise in foolhardiness which is what it really was. My personality was rigged to think it physically invincible so imagine my surprise to find out that was not the case in August of 1926!

If I could take all the bad driving back I would as I endangered others on many occasions. However, in the big picture my recklessness gave me a counterpoint to work with and indeed that element was integrated into some of the roles I played. Quicksilver, this daring-do was also present in some of my other adventures, those of a sexual variety in particular."

33. Over the years a number of books have been written about you and your life. Any observations you want to share?

"Some of them have been breathless, hurried if you will, but what they all brilliantly accomplished was to keep my name alive and, reflexively, further contemplation of that which is love."

34. Why the static, at times, among some of your fans in their relationships with each other?

"One of my goals is to foster cooperation and I do bring disparate people to the table, each of whom somehow believes that he or she has the inside track, understands who and what I was. Well, I do beg to differ. The constructive angle here, however, is communication. That I and my life are so discussed has the ultimate effect of self-examination, most importantly where the topic of love is concerned. This comports with what I am doing now, with you and others, which is lots of communicating.

There are implacable differences among the fans but they all love what I inspire, what my screen characters impart: a vibration that is commensurate with life itself."

35. What did cigarettes do for you?

"A trivia question of sorts, yet not. The cigarette was a sign of sophistication in the milieu of those times, the Hollywood days in particular, and for me it was a steadying influence, I suppose drug of choice. I do not endorse this vice. It was simply something my Rudy self latched onto never to let go."

36. Would you care to comment on any of the films made thus far that attempt to depict your life, and/or actors who portrayed you?

"Most have been farcical, very general, and supremely off the mark in terms of actual narrative and its accompanying emotion. Cash in, cash out, that was the prime motivation rather than being instructive, creating a learning instrument, for that is what my life was: examples of being and not being, the sum of which were the choices I made.

The short film Ballerini wrote (*referring to "Goodnight Valentino" and actor/director Edoardo Ballerini*) had some thought given to it and therefore exhibited aspects of my erstwhile reality but the big budget and especially the most recent, made for Italian TV, are really soap operas diverging from the truth at almost every turn.

Anthony Dexter, an interesting man who could not shake his resemblance to me, did bring some verve to the role. (*He played Rudy in the 1951 biopic "Valentino," a Columbia Picture.*) The real movie of my life has yet to be made!"

37. What are some of your fondest memories?

"There are so many. The first time I saw the Champs-Elysées, the first paycheck I received which spoke, symbolically, to personal worth, getting my first dog, watching a bird alight on the balcony of our apartment in Castellaneta, riding my horse in the Hollywood Hills and surveying the landscape, sun ablaze ~ nothing to do with fame or being a movie star. Know this: it is the simple things we most remember when reviewing our lives and the other observation I will make is that nature or some aspect of love will almost always play a part."

38. How would you describe what you are doing now, your life in the Great Beyond?

"I actively monitor a variety of circumstances acting as guide and mentor for what I would say is an incalculable number of people. My skill is to reflect love, and in so doing, help them grasp that quality in themselves. To love is the greatest achievement anyone can ever attain, fully and without reservation. My own growth figures in as I am a student (as are all of you) in the life I currently lead. In immersing myself in these activities, my attention is both focused and diffused as each experience must filter, inbound and outbound. This is a brilliant place to embrace, my friends, and I adore being of service."

39. Can you elaborate on how you look into the lives of the people you have a mutual agreement with to mentor?

"What a charming question! You could liken the process to my keeping an eye on countless screens, monitors you call them when associated with computers. And I have the ability in this state of being to glance and almost instantaneously understand the totality of what is taking place then interact, to the extent I can given the properties of the Veil, with that individual, someone with whom I have truck, karmic or otherwise. In many of these interactions I have merely agreed to be an advisor, again with their consent."

40. How did other life-times impinge upon your experiences as Rodolfo? In other words, what did they bring to the table?

"I was prepared to be in the public eye as I had had lots of prior experience in that regard. I was also born with a bit of the rogue and rake in my DNA, which I then had to temper, alchemize if you will, into more constructive frames of reference commensurate with what I represent: facets of love, love energy, and the sense of accomplishment and completion they engender. On a micro level I was gifted with certain qualities and know-how which would prove invaluable, my rapport with horses for example. This is equally true for all of you. Each of us has our gifts and they are frequently based on what we have already known or done."

41. Which of your talents would you have liked to explore further?

"Singing. I could have improved my voice with lessons but remained in amateur status. Those two recordings (*the Kashmiri Song and El Relicario*) were an attempt to be serious but I was truly not prepared. The mitigating factor is that they are the sole surviving record of my voice, its tone and intonation patterns. A sweet note to end on! And also I did want to try my hand at art. Roads not taken!"

42. Every year, for the past 87, there has been a Memorial Service in your honor at Hollywood Forever Cemetery in Los Angeles on August 23rd, the date of your death. Do you care to comment on your participation?

"I have been present in spirit at each one, showering those who would receive it with love, love dust, if you will. I was certainly both fêted and well-remembered but it is not my former personality that seeks adulation but rather the soul, as representative of love. So in essence it is love they honor, in all its iterations, as much as the man Rodolfo. That said, I am eternally grateful to those who plan and execute these celebrations every year. They do all of us great service."

43. What do you want your legacy to be?

"To wake people up, open their eyes to any number, or string, of possibilities, mostly found through examining their own hearts and feelings. If a symbol ever were mine, it would be a heart shape, the outline. I also want to convey that you are we and we are you, which is to say that there is a universality of experience that every person can relate to, the sense of being AT ONE."

VALENTINO FILMOGRAPHY

(Rudy reflects on his extant films, plus three others.)

"PATRIA" ~ Pathé, 1917 (*as an extra*)

"The day Ithaca came to me! The director of this serial deigned to film a scene in New York City, to capture the atmosphere and allow Irene Castle, the star, to dance in a milieu she knew quite well. Though short notice, I had been informed and made it a point to be present, to extol myself in the background, and mingle with the crowd. How I would have liked to dance also, to preen a bit upon the silver screen! Not really an acting experience, yet it was ~ an exercise in **fare la bella figura**." (*Making a good impression.*)

"ALL NIGHT" and "A SOCIETY SENSATION" ~ Universal Pictures, 1918

The first time Valentino was a featured player. Though not yet fully aware of the power he was able to project in subsequent films, Rudy displays his ease in every frame of these outings, both of which were released long before he was catapulted to fame in "The Four Horsemen of the Apocalypse."

"My adolescence, at least in the movie industry, is represented by these pictures. I was thrilled to have a top billing in two Carmel Myers films, at a time when her name and reputation were known. A stroke of good fortune, and I embraced the experience! If you take a careful look at my acting here, it was obviously not nuanced yet still there were hints of that. Some pratfalls, yes, but I perfected my sense of timing in these confections, for that is what they were, simple **divertissements** (*amusements*) meant to make audiences smile, maybe laugh out loud a little too. I had paid attention to the great comedians of the day and how they approached their work. Then, when offered the opportunity, I applied my own spin and spin I did. In fact, a couple of the scenes were breath-taking, quite literally, like when I fell into a barrel of rainwater or had to pretend to be cramped up while swimming in the ocean. Carmel was easy to work with, a good sport, game for the physicality her roles often required. Beach boy? Not at all though I did pull that scene out of the hat, made it appear convincing. (*re: being rescued from drowning by Carmel's character.*)

These are not Valentino films that people commonly speak of but my exuberance was on display, aspects of character that never came fully out of the box on other occasions. Fondly I remember the details of all those entrances and exits ~ in and out, we ran ourselves ragged while having fun. Sun-kissed shoots, through a 'Universal' lens!"

"A MARRIED VIRGIN" ~ Maxwell Productions, 1918

"In the spring of my career, when the flowers were barely starting to bud, I was offered a part in a modern melodrama as the heavy, or rather **il furbo** ~ the crafty one with plans to manipulate most of the other characters ~ the role, or person, who perhaps most reflected dollar signs. So I was to project the old world here, colliding with the new, noblesse, a Count confronting crassness but in reality using naïve women for his own purposes. I summoned my fantasies and dug deep inside to inquire how a nefariously inclined Rudy might act within the confines of that script. I was also called upon to be dispassionate, chilly, cunning, perfunctory, a man whose avarice knows no bounds, cad, **roué**. (*Libertine.*) Not terribly appealing attributes!

Upon review, however, there was frankness, a matter-of-fact quality in the plot, creaky though it was ~ passion, obsession ~ unusual for the time and in that sense sophisticated. Dark corners ~ every character was tested and male/female roles twisted and stretched. Though a little young to be a world-weary jaded gentleman, I gave it a go, adopted my own mannerisms to imply the sinister. Again, not a redeeming character, that Count, thoroughly a bounder. On the other hand, I got to play with stereotypes and perceptions of power. I also functioned as a key on set, a cohesive factor, shall we say, when not in front of a camera.

The underbelly, sunny side up, is how I would define this plot, base instincts examined and realigned. Everyone grew and this film got me more opportunities to be a heavy, prepared me for what was to follow. Sexual mores, the perception of affection versus the real thing, as personified by the ingénues: the heart of the matter.

My hands, in particular, served me well in this role as demonstrated in the piano playing scene when I was attempting to quell the trepidations of my newly acquired wife. My hands, those hands, took on a life of their own in

Valentino pictures, a subliminal effect. My way of saying that no matter what my character's predicament, all was truly well and as it should be. A curiosity, this film ~ of its time, and in the present!"

"A DELICIOUS LITTLE DEVIL" ~ Universal Pictures, 1919

"This piece of fluff was conceived of as a 'Mae Murray' picture, a showcase for her talents, which were being noticed at the time. She slogged her way through the script in the sense that she mugged shamelessly for the camera on the premise people thought her cute, which she was. So, there was truth to this. And I got to play an **ingénu**, the guy, in this case, no villain, no exotic, but rather someone named Calhoun who almost effortlessly became enamored of her charms. And Mae was charming, no doubt, much more so in person than when submerged in any character. Mae Murray, a rather alliterative name, don't you think? That was the point! Also, a touch of the blarney, the Irish, so people could relate. Were her performance skills, dance in particular, so great? No, but the gusto with which she strove to portray her role overrode any weaknesses she might have displayed.

We, she and I, were thick as thieves during this shoot, Mae always in my ear, and relating in other intimate ways also. My role was not stellar yet it gave me an opportunity to develop different aspects of my screen persona, to be more forthright and earnest, to be the 'boy' though a wealthy one at that. Interesting that the same actor played my father or was a father in several of my films. We dovetailed well, he and I, and our physical dissemblance played no part in that, was not a factor.

Mae, the spitfire, chewing gum on set, what her character bespoke! Universal cranked this one out fairly quickly yet there was enough detail, adequate meat on the bones. A modest hit, and the title was intriguing!"

"VIRTUOUS SINNERS" ~ Pioneer Films, 1919

"Norman's film (*Norman Kerry*) was a trifle at best but I did have an opportunity to meet Wanda Hawley who later would be what I would call a reluctant leading lady ~ reluctant because she did not see "*The Young Rajah*" as likely to further her career. Norman got me this work at a time when mine was still in the nascent stage. And I was grateful, though my screen time limited ~ what they call a bit part. The good thing is it was against type to a certain extent, a poor person instead of a count. Though in existence, very few have ever seen this effort and again my contribution was negligible.

The funny thing about many of the films of this era is that they often had catchy titles which, even though they had little to do with the plot, might intrigue audiences to purchase a ticket. In this case at least, one could relate the title to the story, albeit tangentially. That said, the shoot was a blur and basically I just showed up; very little acting was called for."

"THE EYES OF YOUTH" ~ Equity Pictures Corporation, 1919

"Had I not made this picture I might not have been chosen to play Julio, perhaps my most important role. It was fortunate that I had worked with Clara before. (*Clara Kimball Young.*) Actually it was she who suggested me for the part, someone she felt comfortable with but, according to her, could lend a nefarious note to the proceedings. And I was indeed unctuous, the operator who got paid to stage a performance and sully her character's reputation. The role was tiny yet intense and I vowed to make the best of it, to leave my mark on the viewers. A morality play that had a certain degree of effectiveness, at least presenting conundrums that were commensurate with the times, the changing mores we were all noticing in 1919.

I found Clara to be an accomplished actress and I counted myself lucky to have a key scene with her. And, the rest is history! June Mathis studied my performance and, based on what she saw, lobbied Metro to hire me for a major motion picture, the ground-breaking "*Four Horsemen.*"

I am forever grateful to this film, this part, which showed how I could 'be' ~ my versatility, with any script. Cabaret parasite, that's how I was billed. The most unpleasant role I ever had, despicable, and I had already tread those boards before. Lots of practice playing heavies in my salad days, but this was done to prepare me for what was yet to come."

"AN ADVENTURESS/ISLE OF LOVE" ~ Republic, 1920

"Well, I did have to have at least one exploitative picture in my repertoire! I took the job, not out of interest in the story or script, but because it came at a low point in my finances. And, it was another opportunity to play a continental type which for me was like falling off a log. I was amused by Eltinge, (*Julian Eltinge*) not in the least threatened by his ability to project the opposite sex. He did it well and people were entertained. My scenes were short and they became even more truncated as those who owned the prints tried to cash in repeatedly by re-cutting and re-issuing the film. I did have some scenes with Virginia Rappe who I found delightful, and the film's initial release, of course, preceded her untimely death. What an effervescent woman she was!

So this film, as poorly made as it was, did offer a few tidbits and visual confrontations, meaning audience sensibilities were challenged ~ racy for the time, though in an unsuccessful way."

"THE WONDERFUL CHANCE" ~ Selznick Picture Corporation, 1920

"Quite a misnomer as my character does not get the opportunity he hoped for: to ransom the Duke, or rather the faux Duke, not clear which. So, a small part this one, with little face time, and most would agree upon viewing this footage that it was one of my most inconsequential appearances on the silver screen. I snarled a bit, almost twisted my moustache, as would any tin-horn villain, but I did also add a bit of swag to the role, my own little touches.

The plot was relatively non-existent, only the roughest of outlines, and really low budget. My interactions with the other characters were minimal so the less said about this picture probably the better. It did provide me with a new suit, however, and a few extra coins in my pocket. Mundane, no, more than mundane, commonplace might be the operative word for describing this endeavor, silly too!"

"STOLEN MOMENTS" ~ American Cinema
Corporation, 1920

"In retrospect, this title was most apt. Perhaps we stole a
little time from the audience, also from our own careers!
This film was filler, nothing much but fluff, very little plot
or story, especially in the footage that exists today. I did
relish being in Florida for the shoot and, of course, that I
was hired, at this time, to star in *The Four Horsemen*" is
etched in my memory!

My co-star was a game woman who did not have a lot of on-
camera experience. She was at ease in public, however, had a
singing career, and I would say she did adequately portray
her character's distress. Again, a rudimentary screenplay and
the director only wanted caricatures; in fact, he sought them
out. If I ever phoned in a performance, this was it. Perhaps
no accident that a telephone niche had such prominence in
the script!

Not much sheen here although my carriage was forthright,
as always, and I did get an opportunity to be elegant, though
reprehensible. The final foray, this was the last of my villain
roles!"

"THE FOUR HORSEMEN OF THE APOCALYPSE" ~
Metro Pictures, 1921 (*based on the novel by Vicente Blasco-
Ibáñez and adapted for the screen by June Mathis.*)

"There are multiple layers to this experience, and I shall do
my utmost to honor each and every one! A first on many
levels, this *Four Horsemen* ~ the first Mathis screenplay of
that particular author's prodigious work, June's masterpiece,
and what was to be the apogee of my career. Indeed, such

heights were achieved and there were incredible soars, by everyone in the cast. And not only that, this film was the first instance of million dollar box office!

We speak, on stage, of hitting your mark. Well, everyone went beyond that. Let's describe it as pitch perfect. We heard celestial music as we filmed, spoke to each other, and acted in every scene. It was as though the Divine was present, thoroughly permeating each soul without any impediment of personality or desire. Even our director, Rex, he who thwarted me later in our next work of art, did indeed manifest with speed. He was in the flow, illumined, I would say, with the glow of glory, for we were imparting an epic, a tale of two cities, two worlds, the old and the new, and the conflicts inherent in each.

I could not believe my good fortune to have a leading role in such a production, one of this stature, which blazed trails for me in terms of popularity and money. We were family, that cast, for as long as the shoot did last. No strife, no egos getting in the way, pure id translated to the essence of each character. Alice Terry's angelic demeanor came into play, as it did in our second outing, but here she used it to communicate her anguish: duty versus passion, and how those two forces tore her character apart/asunder.

My dreams were unrivaled while in the throes of playing Julio, who I owned more perhaps than any of my subsequent characterizations with the exception of Juan. There was strength in Julio, stubbornness, gumption, which he used to pursue his goals, his journey, from languid fop to focused warrior. Here is my finest work in front of a camera, and a story still as relevant as it was in 1921. The scope and spectacle are truly amazing and I remain so grateful to have partaken of this magical project. Thank you, June, Rex, Vicente! A perfect confluence of people and alignment! **Grazie mille!**" (*Many thanks!*)

"CAMILLE" ~ Metro Pictures, 1921 (*based on the novel "La Dame aux Camélias" by Alexandre Dumas, fils, and adapted for the screen by June Mathis.*)

"What a graceful rendering of a famous novel, one that is cherished in circles of good literature! June once again was in her element, delivering a captivating screenplay.

I was both honored and delighted to play Armand. Yes, I was slightly wary of the famous Nazimova, her moods, her demands, but I was also intrigued, not only with the project but with its set and costume designer, the woman who was to become my second wife, Natacha Rambova. She put a decidedly modern spin on the proceedings with her very deco/streamline sets and up-to-date costumes, especially Nazimova's gowns. I was more traditional in my appearance but she was a confection. Madame, as she was often called, was never more vulnerable, more tragic in her affectations.

The shoot, I recall, had a short schedule but we labored diligently, intoxicated with the creativity of what we hoped to accomplish. I could be bitter that some of my most nuanced work did not make the final cut as Nazimova had sway but I'm still proud of my efforts. Of course, we did have to concentrate on our rapport with each other. Though she was no stranger to men, Madame sometimes pursued other interests which I found both amusing and a challenge. I think we came off well together, emoting appropriately ~ a palpitating longing, and all the while, during my close-ups with Nazimova, I saw Natacha in my mind's eye. She hovered on the set and that was more than fine with me!

This picture opened to mostly positive reviews and was seen as moving the goal posts in terms of what could be offered visually and how a traditional story could be depicted in modern times. **Je l'ai aimé beaucoup, et nous avons parlé français sur la scène,** (*I liked it a lot and we spoke French on set*) while the cameras were rolling. **Jolis souvenirs!** (*Wonderful memories!*)

By the way, Nazimova was a creature of invention: image projections and exoticism incarnate, at least in 1921. Metro had doubts about this film, its efficacy, yet they were pleased with the results because it got people talking and made them some money!"

"THE CONQUERING POWER" ~ Metro Pictures, 1921 (*based on the novel "Eugénie Grandet" by Honoré de Balzac and adapted for the screen by June Mathis.*)

"Well, there certainly was a lot of excess around that shoot, from the feverish visions of Rex Ingram, which translated in numerous ways, to the actual props that stood in for Père Grandet's gold. A somewhat flat effort though the premise was worthwhile. Alice (*Alice Terry, Ingram's wife*) and I did know how to dovetail, meaning we were very complimentary on an energetic level. And, she was very adept at displaying innocence. I, on the other hand, was the **roué,** (*someone steeped in debauchery*) personifying the height of excess from the other side of the coin. As opposed to my uncle in the film, I was both spendthrift and libertine.

I did find the big party scene amusing, especially certain
images, and there were all sorts of little details I added,
sometimes much to Rex's consternation or chagrin. A
potboiler in some sense yet the basic story, the redeeming
quality of love, overshadowed the proceedings. Metro brass
kept their hands off this one so the final product was mostly
Rex's, petulant as he sometimes could be. The script was a
little creaky - perhaps not June's best work. Virile I was in
that part though dandified too. My comeuppance forced me
to re-assess, and the purity of love I realized with Alice's
character smote me, in the best way possible. I was
transfigured and transformed by the love of a good woman.
Gold, on the other hand, was an instrument of death, as it
actually often is, in one manner or another."

(*This film is also referenced in the essay on eyes in "Valentino
Speaks."*)

"In one of my films, I wore a monocle. Very fitting because
in that role my character's sight was limited due to the
circumstances of his birth. However, with the help of love,
the conquering power, he eventually learned to use both of
his eyes to see what was before him."

"THE SHEIK" - Paramount, 1921 (*based on the novel by
Edith Hull.*)

"The imprint that continues its effect, even to this day! Not
my favorite role, but in some respects perhaps the most
'stellar' of my career!

Have you ever seen a simpering Sheik? Neither have I so
when Paramount proposed I take the part, and even though
Natacha thought very little of it, I was determined to give it

a go, to imbue what Mrs. Hull had written with flesh and bone. As we began to shoot, I soon realized that the script, and director, were steering me toward stereotype, I, the Arab, who apparently was actually a European. Agnes Ayres was a peach and I mean that in the fullest sense of the lingo of that time. She fulfilled the other half of the puzzle and created, along with my efforts and character, great congruency with the original story. Yes, we were faithful to it but, of course, with certain liberties and truncations. Fun it was to embrace the accoutrements of that role ~ blades, daggers, baggy pants, turbans and the like ~ rather exotic the whole enterprise for we were breaking new ground, cracking the code, the one that guaranteed that racial divisions stay intact. So that is why, from my current vantage point, I see this role as having been significant, a foot in the door for cross-cultural and ethnic connections ~ make them more palatable to the public, expand consciousness.

The part called for great physicality, and I was more than ready to oblige. My prowess with horses and animals of all types came into play, added yet another ingredient to the mix. Did I over-do a few scenes? Of course, friends, as seen through your lenses! But it was appropriate at the time, for what we wanted to accomplish, and what the director required. Color had a role in this film too as certain scenes were given greater heft by the addition of tinting, the sands of the desert made more inviting perhaps than they would ordinarily be. An unexpected hit for Paramount, this film, and a signature role, as it turned out, what I could not foresee at the time.

Hard to believe but there were aspects of this film that were challenging for me ~ a little touch of priggery, superciliousness, in a few scenes when I spurn Agnes' character which was not at all commensurate with my personal style and therefore somewhat hard to pull off. But I did, and effectively enough so that no one noticed I had to work at it.

Women's fantasies were raised, albeit tickled by the premise of this script, and enchantment reigned. Once upon a time, this film was on everyone's mental screen and in a gaggle of cinemas too, a box-office champ of 1921. Quite a gambit! And, I became elevated, risen as a star. I suppose you could say I was truly hatched!"

"MORAN OF THE LADY LETTY" ~ Paramount, 1922

Rudy, what is your favorite movie and how do you remember it?

"Actually I had several but will pick one today to discuss that is often overlooked in my lexicon of performances. Paramount wanted a hit so they came up with an offbeat story in the form of Moran. Do you think the title character was written as a lesbian? No, but as a woman doubtful that a man could fulfill her, at least not the kind that frequented her father's ship. An interesting pastiche, Moran! I had to tip her over, so to speak, make her suppler, and encourage her to be open to love. This I did and I stretched in my role as did Dorothy (*Moran was played by Dorothy Dalton*) in hers. We were pals and conveyed that fact in the scenes we shared. I got her, or rather my character got her, to crack open the door, the one that leads to the heart ~ where passion lies, sweet and artfully constructed. Out of my character's element too; actually both of our characters were 'at sea' by dint of being together, of attempting to be a couple.

118

I felt carefree in this role, like I did not have to prove a thing. The physicality came easy. I relished the fight scenes, and there was a moral: even odd ducks find love, and tenderness is afoot in the strangest of circumstances. Life-changing events, that's what took place in *"Moran."* Audiences did not appreciate this film at the time but in retrospect we certainly could have improved on some of the details.

Salt of the earth meets a salt of the sea, or playboy meets working girl, a theme as old as the pyramids. There was some sadness too, wistfulness, as both characters are a little out of the mainstream in relation to their peers. Moran and Ramón had that in common. Dandy goes to sea and finds out he loves it, also loves a girl who is rather strange for the most part, definitely not the lacy sort or the landlubbing kind. The villains were fun too, broad strokes. Certainly not a masterpiece yet on some levels instructive; this was *"Moran of the Lady Letty."*

"BEYOND THE ROCKS" ~ Paramount, 1922 (*based on the novel of the same name by Elinor Glyn.*)

"One of the lighter efforts of my Hollywood days, where I was engaged, given the part to toy with my celebrity, as was, and also did, Gloria Swanson.

Dear Gloria, what a sparkling soul, that eternal twinkle in her eye! How fortunate I saw myself, being cast with someone of her stature, perhaps the lead female at Paramount in those now seemingly remote times. A series of 'set pieces' that film, strung together by wispy wires, what we know as plot. High society romp, an excuse for both of us to be clothes horses! Costume changes galore! Style-setting we were, gallant was I, with Gloria's character, furiously kissing her hand but also suavely disguising that ardor. She, and I, really enjoyed certain aspects of that screenplay ~ the social whirl and the exoticism implied by our coupling. Scandalous at the time it was and just a bit juicy. Marrying in haste, or for money, ends up laying waste. Trite perhaps, but true! And, Gloria knew, too! Savvy she was! We both joked when not on camera, had some flippant moments. What a grande dame! I have nothing but the utmost respect for her ~ as a woman, as an actor!

Loved the in-studio scene where I rescued her on the snowy cliff, and the French flashback with its incarnational reverberations and import. An excellent way to read the entrails of our connection ~ as characters, of course! **Parfois, nous avons parlé français sur la scène, pour mieux décaler nos efforts.** (*Sometimes we spoke French on set, in order to better bring forth our efforts.*)

Paramount almost had a big hit here and the film did do reasonably well but it needed polishing, better continuity. Natacha dressed me to the nines, plus fours, and tuxes too. Such were the social circles depicted. So glad this film was revived and people were able to see it aglow, lo, so many years after the fact. It was rumored that Gloria and I had rapport. Yes, that was true. We giggled at our fame and success while being faithful to what the public expected us to do.

The message was turbulence in the water and barriers such as rocks can have some pretty startling results. Unexpected consequences, unforeseen conclusions always lie, just beyond the rocks."

"BLOOD AND SAND" ~ Paramount, 1922 (*based on the novel by Vicente Blasco-Ibáñez and adapted for the screen by June Mathis.*)

"Let us take a good look at "*Blood and Sand*" perhaps the gutsiest of my films ~ in more ways than one. My character is Juan, an everyman lost in the woods of his own making. He has certain dreams which involve escaping the abject poverty of his clan and their chosen profession, **zapateros**, shoemakers as you call them in Spanish. His father is deceased so that firm hand is nowhere to be seen. His mother does her best with a slightly recalcitrant, devil-may-care son. But Juan, like so many men, puts women on a pedestal, more perhaps than he ought, and this is both his salvation and curse. He uses the male energy of his being to interact with nature, with brute force represented in the person of the bull, a literal dance with death though it's really a metaphor for life, a dance for all time.

In the course of the film, Juan pursues his dreams which, in some cases, need to be refined. He is confused by his attraction to a woman of the world, Doña Sol, yet he perseveres with his wife, that all-too-angelic soul, as depicted in the film. Most men do not have contrasts drawn so sharply in their lives but this is a morality play. That is how I saw it at the time and the way that most in the audience perceived it too, a medieval morality play with the options writ large. The obsession, the blind obedience, the unquestioning nature of my character, Juan, leads to his destruction. And he still lives on, in the hearts of too many in the body. There are women with his qualities also so this film was not just instructive for one sex. He does not really see the consequences of his behavior and in the end suffers from a lack of insight.

Juan is a man of instinct. Good as a rule but, dear readers, our instincts must also be refined, expanded, thought-upon and, at times, released when they no longer serve us. Instinct can be confused with the vagaries of personality. We speak of them in metaphysical circles as guide posts which they are but then comes the necessary reckoning with the big picture, what the soul needs to have happen in a given situation. Sometimes we have contracted to play things out in such a way as would be considered a 'bad' end. Juan's case was one of those. His dream was cut short by his untimely death, a foreshadowing of what occurred in my own life. I, too, like Juan, was stubborn in that I reveled in the realm of the senses, regaled myself with them everyday, sometimes imbibing or satiating myself a bit too much. I loved to eat, also a bit of the grape and, of course, all of the things of the body, the electricity of sex perhaps above all. But these things, while wonderful in and of themselves, can sometimes become a means to an end, literally and figuratively. Juan and I in some ways were like peas in a pod. I loved that portrayal, having the opportunity to step into that role. Tailor-made it was for me.

I became immersed. I was the letter, it was the envelope. We fit together like hand in glove. Juan Gallardo was one of the most salient parts I had as an actor, and this film, though a fable of Spain, continues to be relevant to all times and places. The lesson implicit in the script is that just about any form of gluttony does not pay. It is a perverse instinct that really must be tamed and we can only effectively work on it while in the flesh, where we can see its effects in all their glory. Juan worked with bulls but in a way was a pig, never knowing when to stop, to call a halt to his liaison with Doña Sol, to end his obsession with his virginal wife, to re-assess his over-reliance on physical prowess. If it felt good once, let's do it again; that was his motto. There are times to walk away or change tunes and Juan did not avail himself of those opportunities. And, in a way, neither did I when I inhabited the body known as Rodolfo Valentino.

Juan was also a love, sweet beyond belief in his roguish ways and therefore very attractive to both women in his life. The character presents the parable of saint and sinner.

This script, like all movie scripts, like all definable situations, is a dream, Juan's dream; at least, that is how we are perceiving it in this discussion. We can look at it from many angles including, of course, from the points of view of the other characters and why they chose to participate.

Again, I was perhaps more in sync with this role, both with the broad strokes and little flourishes, than with any other of my relatively brief career in front of the camera. Juan is I and I am Juan ~ not entirely of course, but there are remarkable congruencies."

"THE YOUNG RAJAH" ~ Paramount, 1922 (*based on the novel "Amos Judd" and adapted for the screen by June Mathis.*)

"This was perhaps my most ambitious film in terms of blatant proselytization ~ in a good way, of course! *"The Young Rajah"* was designed, by June Mathis, to open many a door. The plot was a little hoary, not too slick, yet its message was right on the mark in that the screenplay normalized what some of you still see as exotic, or too far-fetched. Amos was a dreamer, yes ~ a seer, a gifted man in terms of being able to manifest with ease. All these are truths and really the norm, rather than exception. So I was modeling spiritual practice here though the story a bit goofy, at least from the viewpoint of critics and some movie-goers. But June had the last word, creative license, and prevail she did!

I did not like this film much at the time, thinking it lacking, but now I find it sublime, uniting what's diverse, elements from everywhere, various cultures and societies. Wanda (*co-star, Wanda Hawley*) was not very accessible, rather perfunctory in her affectation but we were adequate on screen, believable as a couple. And, there were individual moments that sparkled ~ like all the gems in 'La Cave d'Ali Baba.' My tear, the cheers, a young man's fancies! An interesting picturization this film, and in certain scenes really effective, with memorable images searing the imagination. June's quote in one of the inter-titles is notable too so I leave you with that thought."

"Men should be judged not by the tint of their skin

The gods they serve, the vintage that they drink

Nor by the way they fight, or love, or sin

But rather by the quality of thought they think."

POSTSCRIPT:

"As Valentino I started a crusade for better scripts, deciding, at the time, that those routinely being offered me were of inferior quality. Now as I review, each had their good points too. This film for example, a picture that I once considered to be among my least successful, examined intuition and the concept of thought-power, especially as it pertains to creating personal reality. Amos Judd, my character, could see

124

the future for others but, alas, not for himself. Nevertheless, he was always busy creating it anyway. And so it is for all of us. Where would we be without our dreams?"

"MONSIEUR BEAUCAIRE" ~ Paramount, 1924

"Artfully is how I approached this film, which is what Natacha and I had in mind: a big splash, my return to the silver screen after what seemed like a rather lengthy absence. Nice work if you can get it, to play dual roles, fey-ish and foppish though they both were on some level. But, I reveled in the details, got lost in some of them too: **les dentelles** (*laces*) ~ **les mouches** (*beauty marks*) ~ **les perruques** (*wigs.*) **Tout** ça (*all of that*) was a stretch for me personally but at the same time expressed aspects of what my characters wanted to be. The intrigue of the court ~ **le badinage** (*banter*) ~ **les froux** (*flourishes*) ~ **les poux** (*lice*) ~ well, they were all a mash up, blend, a lovely glass of port! Yes, "*Monsieur Beaucaire*" had that aspect to it, decadence, but masking the power that lurked below, under the surface, as personified by the King and court.

Though I jumped at the chance to act **en papillote** (*figuratively, in parchment or curling paper*) I was constrained, as it were, by the weight of the visuals and all that 'de luxe.' The most fun was to be a swordsman, the dashing and daring of my 'real self' as opposed to the barber/confidant. The female characters, I remember, were of the cardboard variety and that was all as it should be. No real connections with my co-stars in this outing, only superficial ones. Funny, no, odd to admit that now! Well, this was an exercise in excess, lots of trappings with a very slight story line to support them, sort of like wet wash hanging from delicate tree limbs. In our efforts to get things 'right,' we missed the big picture, and in making this observation, I mean myself, Natacha, and the director, so blinded by our desire to create a work of art were we.

Many critics panned this film and I would say that the whole of it boils down to one of my least favorites. Top-heavy it was, like the hair pieces we wore and fussy, like the ribbons that festooned our pantaloons. Light and shadow, having a field day! Unfortunately, stories of another century do not always comport well with the current one. Again, what I liked best was the swordplay, my chance to inject a little 'Fairbanks' into the picture. Paramount was sorely disappointed with its performance. Not the right vehicle for my comeback, but quite a few poses! **Un bal masqué** (*a masked ball*) ~ the perfect metaphor!"

"A SAINTED DEVIL" ~ Paramount, 1924

"We can address this film as it was one of my mature efforts. Pieces of it still exist and will come to light as was the case with "*Beyond the Rocks*" ~ in a far distant land, unexpected location. At present, however, it is considered lost.

Rex Beach wrote a gripping story which Paramount then purchased the right to film ~ a tale of vengeance and the wronged party, who in this case was me. I steeled myself to play this role, was very deliberate in my affectation. I even willed myself to look a bit different, to expound with a heavier heart, if you will, as my character was consumed with any number of concerns, his bride spirited away right before his eyes, his due, his trophy, shall we say. This film allowed me to enter a realm I ordinarily did not frequent, that of rage, seeing red. Such base instincts were foreign to my make-up so I had to dig deep and channel what I believed them to be. The reviewers of the day did think, by the way, that I had hit my mark and there was sword play, rather neat costumes and sets too!

There was also a smidgen of redemption afoot in the plot, at every turn, which made audiences sympathetic to Don Alonzo's plight. Nita, once again, (*Nita Naldi*) was the nefarious schemer who wanted me for herself, or rather to satiate her character's most intimate desires. Lovely poses, hers, especially with mantilla! As I contemplate this film now, I think of dance, how two-stepping got me through the melancholy. I spent a good deal of this picture being angry and depressed, but again through the lens of goodness and redemption. What a shame that most of the scenes appear to be gone, dissolved into dust!

Natacha had a hand in some of the details of the production, in particular the costuming. That is why they were so brilliant. My co-stars were all for giving this effort the old college try. A game, we saw our interpretation of the script as an elaborate chess board, necessitating very specific moves, choreography, and intricate steps.

Among my most challenging roles and, to tell the truth, it was not very uplifting for my psyche."

"THE HOODED FALCON" ~ circa 1925

Ruminations on "The Hooded Falcon," the film Rudy and Natacha wanted to make but never did. Ritz-Carlton, a newly-founded studio, signed a contract with them to produce it but later reneged on the deal.

"One of the biggest projects ever, in terms of my former life-time, and it did not come to fruition! What was that all about? This film was a specter, an opium-like dream that Natacha and I bought into. We wanted to elevate public taste, dignify and exemplify, in ways that most Hollywood product of the time did not. "*The Hooded Falcon*" was to be an exercise in **hardiesse** (*daring/boldness/pluck*) which is what would have been required to fully make that leap of faith, the one that was necessary for everyone who was to be involved to get on board, to back it 100%. We, meaning primarily Natacha and I, did make a serious effort but got lost in the details instead of starting with a crisp concept, which we thought would evolve by osmosis if we steeped ourselves in drawings, looks and costumes. Natacha liked to work that way and was successful when there was enough meat on the bones, ample flesh upon which she could drape costumes and use to populate sets.

I wanted this role, this picture, to be my masterpiece, a sterling example of all my creative input, as did she, and because we were quite synchronistic at the time, in a sort of harmonic convergence about this property and the reason for its existence and pursuit, we likely would have succeeded in our goals. Conceptually and with the story line, however, there still were gaps when the plug was pulled on the financial side. Could they have been assuaged, addressed, even become attributes? Most assuredly but we did not have the luxury of a bottomless pit when it came to either money or time. Still, the 'shade' was raised, the ghost, the vision walked and one day someone with Hollywood blood in their veins may want to dust off the idea and make the film we always wanted to – unfinished business, brought to the attention of a new century! Of course, the star should resemble me, at least a little. Why not? That would be fun!

My character was to be a Saracen nobleman, by the way. Ecumenical, there was that element too. This film was intended to inspire and unite, to cause audiences, after the pageantry, intrigue and utter delight to think a bit more, become, themselves, of the Light."

"COBRA" ~ Ritz-Carlton/Paramount, 1925

"A mélange at best, and interestingly it also had elements of the best I had in me to give. Slightly autobiographical as it depicts my interest in times of yore, the world of castles, princes knocking on the door, princesses too, ladies in their finery and plumes gallantly allowing only well-chosen gentlemen in their rooms. I particularly enjoyed the costumed scene, the flashback.

There was pathos in that character, a melancholy man so many could relate to, a world-weary playboy on the lookout for something more complete. And there were flashes of my own sensitivity and sensibility, qualities I specifically wanted to infuse my character with. The script was mundane yet working together we were able to re-frame it, inject a bit of the unexpected into what could easily have been lame. There were still a few groaners but mostly it worked ~ a morality play and an examination of friendship, i.e. how deep can it go? I was a clothes horse in those 'modern times' with my own sense of propriety about the whole affair. And my input with details was perhaps greater than usual as the director was malleable in his make-up, willing to consider adding a few ornamental flourishes.

Count Torriani was an everyman who, after being accosted by a vamp, a cold-hearted and calculating woman, came out of the encounter with a resolve, perhaps to move on, do better, rise to another or perhaps different vibrational pose. As for my co-stars, I found Gertrude Olmstead attractive and she me so we didn't have to act much. We felt comfortable with each other and, of course, Nita (*Nita Naldi*) played the archetype oh so well.

"*Cobra*" was a cautionary tale yet tinged with hope, nonetheless, about letting go of obsessions, whatever form they may take. 'Twas also about what one might do to restore one's honor. Again, we turned a rather dreary screenplay into something sleeker than it might have been in other hands, or lands. Chalk one up for Hollywood! There were flashes of inspiration in that endeavor, from a number of quarters."

"THE BRONZE COLLAR" (*never made, this was to be Rudy's first film at United Artists Pictures ~ circa 1925*)

"Initially I was enthusiastic about this project but came to see it was too formulaic a script, hearty, perhaps, like a good soup but not intricate enough nor would it have been a challenge as an actor. I guess I could compare the role to one Errol Flynn might have been asked to play in his heyday. Though the making of this film had been trumpeted, wiser heads prevailed and it was shelved in favor of "*The Eagle*" ~ a far more astute choice."

"THE EAGLE" ~ United Artists, 1925

"A breath of fresh air is how I saw this picture and my role in it, also a stretch and a chance to redeem my career which was somewhat stagnant prior to its release. A new studio, a rather generous budget, the examination of dual roles, multiple personalities, stereotypes, and the exercise of power ~ for example, the dynamics at play between the Czarina and me. In particular, my character's wiles trumping her ability to be clever and preemptive.

Russian Imperial accoutrements, my goodness, how I loved all that, also the horses, playing an equestrian, working with animals ~ which at times I preferred to my human acquaintances. And this movie marked my initial foray with Vilma Banky, preparing us for the seminal portrayals we both achieved in my final film. This was the penultimate, by the way, and quite a frolic, tongue in cheek, slightly comedic yet with great dash and verve. Love conveyed, especially in the final scenes, tender and moist. We were both crying as we realized how precious each moment is, and that is what I would like viewers to take away, those who watch this footage today. We only have this moment, this space, and the power of love, especially when acknowledged, always carries us through ~ so true!

Friperies (*second hand goods*) ~ I also dabbled with silliness as the tutor, the unconscious and rather unlikeable anti-suitor. This film was a study in contrasts: the political and economic reality of those times as well as the stations of life ~ just a touch of buffoonery too, not so much with my character, more the father and his henchmen. United Artists had a hit on their hands and I was back on top! Breezy ~ if there is one word to describe my performance, that would be it! **Grazie mille!** (*Many thanks!*) This was one of my favorite roles, a romp from beginning to end ~ studied careening!"

"SON OF THE SHEIK" ~ United Artists, 1926

"This film was the zenith of my career and strangely also the nadir, though I did not know that when it made its début.

I had had several years to contemplate the persona of the Sheik, how he was depicted, and how I wanted him to be remembered. In fact, I had cogitated on it a fair amount so when United Artists broached the idea, my resistance to a reprise had already dissipated. I was fully conscious of what I set out to accomplish which was to add other dimensions to that character, to soften him as well as toughen him up. Ahmed was at home in the desert, also comfortable in a lady's boudoir. He projected sex appeal and a sense of vulnerability, strength yet remorse, unabashed delight with a touch of the pensive. He was a study in contrasts and to that mix I added a double, myself, or rather Ahmed, as an older man, what I might have become had my own life script not been so short. Fun to picture the Sheik at fifty, apply old age make-up, examine myself in the mirror! This character was truly a kaleidoscope, refractions upon reflection, if you will.

The details were important. I added my own possessions and I also bought things expressly for them to appear on camera. My sensibility as an ancient Egyptian, for once so was I, came into play, the knowing that the desert, which in this case was in Arizona, could be quite hospitable. There was a fated aspect to the production, a storied quality that quickly became evident once the shoot had commenced. Vilma shown in her role; she sparkled like a jewel. This film had everything: adventure, intrigue, love ~ all without anyone being aware of what was soon to become the full force of its impact at the time. It is perhaps the one effort of mine people most remember, not fans but the general public.

Brains and brawn, laced with heart. I have fond memories of this film and its many devices, the sense of freedom it engendered, in actor and audience alike.

Riding off into the sunset, one of the greatest clichés ever yet perhaps the most effective, the **grand dénouement!**" (*Final resolution.*)

(One of Rudy's favorite roles: Ramón in "Moran of the Lady Letty" ~ Paramount, 1922)

LESSONS LEARNED

"From my current vantage point, I can examine the contents of the 'toy' box, those elements that individually or collectively made an impact on my life, the parts of the whole. This shall also be the case for you, as it's an experience that awaits us all!

What, indeed, did I learn during the time I occupied the body known as Rodolfo Valentino? Well, circumstances, of my own choosing of course, offered myriad opportunities to hold myself up to a mirror, psychological ones as well as those of the every-day variety. My chore, at least one out of many, was to confront vanity as I was meticulous, some would say, about my presentation. To place less importance on that while at the same time preening before multiple cameras was quite the challenge! And yet I did meet it, was able to attach less weight, at least mentally, to the **bella figura** concept so ingrained in my home country.

Ego was another stumbling block, not to become too inebriated with either my fame or those who wanted to sleep with me, or merely spend time in my presence.

Ah yes, we are each endowed with a whole slate of personal quirks and ticks (I would also call them shticks) that must be attended to. My tendency to pursue casual intimacy was one of those yet on the other side of that coin the experiences themselves and what I garnered from them were all of prime importance.

As Rodolfo, my armor was my smile. It was genuine, of course, but also, at times, a means to an end, an adjunct to ego.

Humility, I was made more aware of what a sterling quality it actually is.

As I review, what was it that I knew? That I should tread the boards, step onto the stage, take the spotlight, and use those means to emulate and embody love, to exude it however I could. This was my gift to the world."

~ *RUG*

AFTERWORD

"I speak because I can ~ to, with, and through a number of people via various vibratory modalities, each according to their individual wants, needs and, most importantly, life scripts as there must always be mutual agreement for this to occur. In so doing, I play many parts, the most significant of which are mentor, teacher, and confidant.

That said, do not be tempted to place me on a pedestal. I am, and was, a man with foibles and the occasional blind spot. Yet I implore you to use my experiences, to be instructed and informed by them to help you in your journeys, assess your own adventures. **Vi voglio bene, tutti quanti!**" (*I love all of you!*)

~ *Rudolph Valentino*

AFTERWORD, BIS

O nly rarely does anyone reveal his or her true self, what really makes them tick. Here we have Rudy pulling back the curtain posthumously, showing us his heart. Ladies and Gentlemen, the memoirs of Rudolph Valentino!

~ Wayne Hatford

PARTIAL BIBLIOGRAPHY

"*Rudolph Valentino – The Silent Idol*" by Donna Hill - a pictorial re-cap of Valentino's trajectory, as a man, and star. Not only are the photos spectacular, the accompanying narrative is replete with interesting nuggets and highlights.

"*Dark Lover*" by Emily Leider - the most complete Valentino biography to date.

"*Rudolph Valentino: The Early Years, 1895 – 1920*" by Jeanine Villalobos - Valentino's great grand-niece examines the first 25 years of her famous relative's life through the prism of family archives, including letters in Rudy's own hand. Currently available only in dissertation format.

Of course, there are many other books that either directly or tangentially explore Rudy's life and legacy. I leave it to you to decide which ones most appeal, as all have something to offer, food for thought. Happy reading!

OTHER BOOKS BY WAYNE HATFORD

"*Valentino Speaks: The Wisdom of Rudolph Valentino*" ~ metaphysical primer, a treasure trove of useful information.

"*Going for Excelsior: Thriving in Seniorhood*" ~ strategies for successfully negotiating one's 'senior' years, a blueprint for active living.

"*Letters from Janice: Correspondence with the Astral Plane*" ~ a dear friend recounting her experiences with the transition called 'death.'

INTERNET RESOURCES

www.valentinospeaks.com

www.rudolph-valentino.com

ABOUT THE AUTHOR

Wayne Hatford is a medium, teacher and author dedicated to bridging the gap between the physical and non-physical worlds. Born in the Midwest, he has lived on both coasts of the US while also traveling extensively, spending significant amounts of time in Chile, France, Spain and Italy. It is Italy, however, the birthplace of Rudolph Valentino, where he feels a special rapport and, in scholarly pursuits, has visited multiple sites associated with the 'Great Lover.' Wayne speaks French, Italian, Spanish and English, the languages in which Valentino himself was conversant. As a result, he was able to provide Rudy with the perfect palette, allowing him to share his thoughts with the same texture and vibrancy he employed during his last incarnation.

A life-long student of metaphysics and transformation whose other books, "*Letters from Janice: Correspondence with the Astral Plane*," "*Going for Excelsior: Thriving in Seniorhood*" and "*Valentino Speaks: The Wisdom of Rudolph Valentino*" are also available via Amazon.com, Wayne has both been a public school teacher and worked in the antique auction industry as a personal property appraiser.

Wayne Hatford now resides in San Francisco, California. For updates and more information, please visit www.valentinospeaks.com.